OPEN
SECRETS

Also by Walt Anderson

The Age of Protest
Campaigns: Cases in Political Conflict
Politics and Environment: A Reader in Ecological Crisis
Politics and the New Humanism
Evaluating Democracy (with Joseph Allman)
Therapy and the Arts
A Place of Power

OPEN SECRETS

*A Western Guide to
Tibetan Buddhism*

WALT ANDERSON

KUM-NYE ILLUSTRATIONS BY
ADELE ALDRIDGE

The Viking Press / New York

LIBRARY OF CONGRESS CATALOGING IN PUBLICATION DATA
Anderson, Walt, 1933–
Open secrets.
Includes index.
1. Buddhism. I. Title.
BQ7604.A5   294.3'923   79-12017
ISBN 0-670-52712-2

Printed in the United States of America
Set in CRT Palatino

Acknowledgments

Dharma Press: From *Crystal Mirror*, Vol. IV (1975), Dharma Publishing, Emeryville, California. © 1975 Dharma Publishing.

Hutchinson Publishing Group Limited: From *The Wisdom of Buddhism*, by Christmas Humphreys.

Science and Behavior Books, Inc.: Reprinted by permission of the editor and the publisher from F. S. Perls, "Dream Seminars." In J. Fagan and I. L. Shepherd (Eds.), *Gestalt Therapy Now*. Palo Alto, California: Science and Behavior Books, 1970.

St. Martin's Press, Inc., and The Bodley Head: From *Buddhism*, by Alexandra David-Neel.

University of California Press (Berkeley): From *The Cult of Tara*, 1973.

Samuel Weiser, Inc.: From *Foundations of Tibetan Mysticism*, by Lama Anagarika Govinda. (New York: Samuel Weiser, Inc., 1978).

Shambhala Publications, Inc., Hutchinson Publishing Group Ltd., Rider & Co.: From *The Way of the White Clouds*, by Lama Govinda.

Shambhala Publications, Inc.: From *The Dawn of Tantra*, by Herbert V. Guenther and Chögyam Trungpa, Copyright © 1975 by Herbert V. Guenther and Chögyam Trungpa. Reprinted by special arrangement with Shambhala Publications, Inc., 1123 Spruce Street, Boulder, Colo. 80302.

Than knowledge of This there is nothing else.
Other than This no one can know.

It is This that's read and This that's meditated,
It's This that's discussed in treatises and old legends.
There is no school of thought that does not take This
as its aim. . . .

SARAHA

Here we seek and find our difficulties, here we seek and find our
enemy, here we seek and find what is dear and precious to us; and it is
comforting to know that all evil and all good is to be found out there,
in the visible object, where it can be conquered, punished, destroyed or
enjoyed. But nature herself does not allow this paradisal state of in-
nocence to continue for ever. There are, and always have been, those
who cannot help but see that the world and its experiences are in the
nature of a symbol, and that it really reflects something that lies hid-
den in the subject himself, in his own transsubjective reality.

C. G. JUNG

Preface

ONE DAY a stranger comes into our village. We have been going about our usual routines—trading and hunting, feuding with other tribes, practicing our rituals—and for a while we stop what we have been doing and gather round the stranger to have a look at him. He is oddly dressed, speaks a language different from our own. We circle about him (or perhaps her—who can tell?), and prod him with our spears, and mutter among ourselves about what we should do. He seems to come in peace; he might be a missionary. Or he might be a merchant of some sort, or the forerunner of an invasion. Maybe we should treat him as a god. Maybe we should kill him and eat him.

IN RELATION to the outsider we will encounter in these pages—Tibetan Buddhism—I stand as one of the locals: I am not a Tibetan or a Buddhist or a professional scholar of Buddhism. This book is my personal prod in the stranger's ribs, my own attempt to tell my fellow villagers what I think Tibetan Buddhism is up to.

Having identified myself as a non-Buddhist, I would like to tell you something about my own background in

Buddhism. I have been interested in it for some time—since 1963, to be exact; I have few other intellectual interests whose origins I can identify with such precision. I can remember the exact day and time it began.

Buddhism came later to me than it did to many other Californians of my generation. I had lived in San Francisco in the late 1950s when everybody was getting excited about Zen, and I viewed all that with benign neglect. It just didn't do anything for me. My intellectual heroes at the time were novelists and philosophers, especially of the European existentialist variety—Sartre, Camus, Kierkegaard, Dostoevsky. I didn't think much of Kerouac and the other Beat writers of the time, and their appropriation of an inscrutable Eastern religion struck me as faintly silly.

Then, in 1963, I was reading a good deal of psychology, and in an anthology I came across an essay entitled "The Ego and Mystic Selflessness," by Herbert Fingarette.[1] * The paper was an attempt to show that there were parallels between the search for emotional health in psychotherapy and the search for enlightenment in Oriental mysticism. The author's sources were psychological case histories and Eastern scriptures, chiefly Zen Buddhist.

About halfway through the essay, I began to understand what the author was talking about, and as I read on, the experience became one of profound insight. And it was much more than just an intellectual experience. I felt a sense of joy, and I also discovered, when I went for a walk to digest the experience, that my sense perceptions had changed, that the world was clearer and brighter than it had been before. It was like having my windshield washed. It was a vivid, energetic feeling, yet not strange, as some chemically induced state might be, not even particularly euphoric; it was a "high," but a peaceful and beautifully balanced one.

As you might expect, I developed a healthy respect for

* Superior numerals throughout refer to chapter notes, which begin on page 216.

Zen as a result of this. I read a lot more about it, and started practicing meditation in an on-and-off fashion. I also searched further in the literature of psychology to see if anybody had anything to say about the kind of experience I had had. I discovered Abraham Maslow's work on the subject of "peak experiences," and later I came across Gestalt therapy and its idea that psychological growth involves making stronger contact with one's own sense perceptions.

As I continued with these explorations over the years, I encountered other Eastern systems—among them yoga and Sufism—and my curiosity broadened beyond the personal quest of understanding my own experience. It became obvious to me, as it must be to everyone by now, that something was happening in this country, that we were being nearly inundated with Oriental religions. The mild Zen frenzy of the 1950s began to look rather small compared to the enlightenment binge of the 1970s. As a political scientist and a professional writer, I was naturally intrigued by all this, and wondered what it all meant to American culture.

Living in Berkeley in the early 1970s, I heard that a Tibetan lama, Tarthang Tulku, had settled here and opened up a Tibetan Buddhist meditation center. That sounded interesting, and I thought that when I could find the time, I would have to look in and see what went on there. As often happens in such matters, Tibetan Buddhism got around to me before I got around to it. American members of the staff at the meditation center, the Nyingma Institute, had read some magazine articles I had written and invited me to sample the center's offerings. They were, of course, practicing the fine old American art of press agentry; the unspoken but clearly understood suggestion was that I might end up writing something about the Institute.

So, practicing that other old American art that is the flip side of press agentry—freeloading—I went to some classes and workshops. This led me into my first true confrontation with Buddhist philosophy. Most of my reading in Zen had

been of Western writers—Alan Watts, Erich Fromm—or
English-speaking Easterners such as D. T. Suzuki. Now, as I
plunged into the Indian and Tibetan scriptures, I began to
deal with material that was written neither by nor for Westerners and that was no doubt difficult even in its own time
and place. Zen had sometimes been difficult, but there was
always a certain clarity about it; even when you didn't understand it, you knew that what eluded you was simple. I
had encountered plenty of complex material in my student
years, of course, had slogged through Aristotle and Kant and
Heidegger and all the quantified craziness of modern social
science; yet none of that was equal in difficulty to sorting out
complex material that came from a culture totally alien to
my own. I was reading the material in translation, but rendering Buddhist philosophy into English does not quite
complete the job of making it accessible to the Western
mind.

I was not the only person who found the Buddhist texts
a bit formidable. There were two kinds of programs offered
at the institute: those concerned with practices (meditation,
exercises, chanting, and so forth) and those concerned with
theory. I sampled both kinds, and observed that there were
always many more people in the practice courses. As many
as fifty people would come for a weekend of meditation, but
the enrollment for a course in Abhidharma theory would
run to about half a dozen, and usually a couple of those
would drop out before it was over.

At some point, during those months of studying Buddhist definitions of mental events, investigating the philosophical differences between the Sarvastivadins and the
Yogacaras, I began to think about writing a book about Tibetan Buddhism, to try to communicate to the intelligent lay
reader some of its basic ideas, because, however foreign and
complex Buddhist philosophy might be, I had found it to
center around some ideas and values that were quite different from our way of looking at things, yet understandable,

and extremely important. I believed—and still do—that
America can use a bit of Buddhism.

My purpose in this enterprise is to make Buddhism a
little more intelligible to Westerners. To do this I have deliberately Americanized it a bit, drawn out its similarities to
themes that run through our own culture. I have also deliberately chosen not to Americanize it all the way, to deprive it
of its strangeness. We need a little of that strangeness.
Human life is lived amid mystery anyway, gliding always on
the edge of the unknown, and it is very dangerous to believe
otherwise. (Keep that thought in mind later on, when I ask
you to try hearing with your eyes.) I don't think we need to
make a fetish of strangeness, though: The Buddhist notion
of the "middle way" applies here, as it does in many cases.

My own way of studying Oriental thought has been to
search out parallels to Western—familiar, safe—ideas,
found in our own arts and sciences and philosophy. It seems
to me that a reasonable way to proceed, in exploring the unknown, is to maintain whatever contact is possible with
what is known. I realize of course that there are adventurers
all about us, spiritual athletes all, who are prepared to throw
the whole heritage of Western culture down the nearest
storm drain and run naked after the next guru. To them I say
good luck, and *bon voyage.*

My form of exploration is learned from my experience
of taking my son to play in Codornices Park in Berkeley,
when he was two or three years old. I would find myself a
good place to lie on the grass in the sunshine, and let him go
his way. He would venture out into that mighty world of
seesaws and swings, where he would discover new friends
and high times and occasional disasters, and, whatever was
happening, every fifteen minutes or so he would come back
to where I was, make contact with the familiar, and then
charge back into the new. Outward, back, outward, back,
goes the pattern of exploration. It seems right to me. Perhaps
something marvelous would have happened to my son if I

had left him alone in the park. I don't know. I never did that to him, and I have never done it to myself.

So you will find us in these pages venturing out into Tibetan Buddhism, coming back to Western civilization to take a look at some comparable ideas, venturing out again. How far you ultimately venture will of course be your own decision. I present a variety of introductory material—basic ideas, beginning exercises and meditation practices—that should give you some understanding of what Tibetan Buddhism is about and some sense of how it feels. You can take it from there.

You are also on your own as to what you choose to believe or not believe. A certain amount of open-mindedness is called for, but I agree with my friend Charles Hampden-Turner's observation that a perpetually open mind is no better than a perpetually open mouth. The ideal, I think, is a healthy mixture of openness and skepticism: a willingness to try something, combined with an unwillingness to believe everything you are told.

I know that many people will find Tibetan Buddhism incompatible with either their religion or their scientifically founded ideas of reality; yet I have met many Christian clergy and American scientists who are deeply involved in Buddhism and not experiencing any inner conflict about that. Buddhism does challenge our Western belief system— it starts out by challenging your idea of who you are, and sooner or later everything else is shaken up as well—but I have personally found that Buddhism both amplifies my appreciation of Christianity and gives me a fresh interest in modern theoretical physics and experimental psychology. So I don't look for Buddhism to replace either our religion or our science; I look for it to participate in a new synthesis of knowledge that will take place as Western civilization assimilates the enormously rich cultural heritage that is now at its disposal.

Most of the exercises described herein are from courses taught at the Nyingma Institute, so naturally they emphasize certain elements that are peculiar to that tradition. Nyingma—which means "old ones"—is the American manifestation of one of the four major sects of Tibetan Buddhism. You might not encounter some of the exercises given in this book—such as the *kum nye*—at other institutions.

The scriptural material from which I draw most of my generalizations about Tibetan Buddhism includes the works of such sages as Milarepa, Naropa, Gampopa, and Longchenpa, all of whom are cited at many points throughout the book, in the best English translations I know of. I took a particular liking to the Tantric poet Saraha, who is quoted at both the beginning and the end of the book, and several places in between.

Saraha, like many of the other sages whose works are basic to Tibetan Buddhism, was an Indian, not a Tibetan. Many of the sources used here are in fact Indian, part of the enormous body of scriptural works that were absorbed into Tibetan Buddhism. I use the Sanskrit rather than Tibetan words for technical terms whenever possible. Tibetan words are used only when we are dealing with a specifically Tibetan concept and there is no precise Sanskrit equivalent that I know of. Where I do use Tibetan words, they are spelled simply and phonetically. I deliberately avoid the spelling form used by many scholars (borrowed from the English system for translating Old Irish), which in attempting to render Tibetan words in English comes up with such productions as *mtshan.nid* and *sdug.bsnal*. These spellings are supposed to enable the reader to get the sound right, but I find them only a little less comprehensible than the original Tibetan.

As you research a subject such as Tibetan Buddhism you are easily drawn off into side alleys, and I especially enjoyed reading the books of the pioneers, the early Western explorers who ventured into Tibet to study its culture and beliefs—L. A. Waddell, W. Y. Evans-Wentz, Alexandra David-Neel. They were a hardy lot, no less interesting than the lamas they befriended and studied. Waddell was an English doctor, an officer in the Indian Medical Service. Stationed at the border town of Darjeeling from 1885 to 1895, he became interested in Tibetan Buddhism and set out to learn about it. His approach was a really stunning piece of anthropological methodology: He bought a temple from the lamas and asked them to show him how it worked. They proceeded to instruct him in their symbols and rites, which he clearly thought were a lot of primitive baloney. The original Buddha, as far as he was concerned, was a rich Indian kid who had some bad luck and couldn't handle it too well: "In his despair, after dreamily sitting for some months cross-legged . . . in shut-eyed introspective 'Meditation,' he believed he had found a new 'Truth'. . . ." Dr. Waddell called Buddhism a "morose nihilistic doctrine," referred to the lamas' most cherished esoteric teachings as "silly secrets," and described their rituals as "contemptible mummery and posturing."[2] He is, as you might expect, not too popular with Tibetan Buddhism's true believers, who think he kind of missed the point of it; but he made a conscientious study of his subject, and his book is worth reading.

Madame David-Neel was a truly formidable lady, a Frenchwoman who traveled through the Orient alone on heroic expeditions (one of her trips lasted fourteen years). She adopted a Tibetan lama as her son and was herself recognized as a lama; she wrote several books and ultimately retired to Switzerland where she lived to be more than a hundred and complained in her later years that people who had heard of her Tibetan exploits were continually disturbing her retirement by coming to her with requests that she hex their enemies or perform other Oriental miracles.

An interesting lot of people, those old searchers, and I am glad to have had an opportunity to get to know them.

BY THE TIME I started exploring Tibetan Buddhism the specific experience that first opened my mind to Buddhism in 1963 had receded into the general background of my life. I had had many other peak experiences since then, and a lot of trough experiences as well. Yet that event—that marvelous breakthrough into a new clarity—was still meaningful to me, and I was pleased to find, finally, a precise description of the state of joyous balance that I had spontaneously slipped into. Tarthang Tulku calls it *shin jong,* the "higher alertness," and talks about it as if he knows the territory.

Acknowledgments

I AM GRATEFUL to Tarthang Tulku, Rinpoche, and to many members of the faculty and staff at the Nyingma Institute who taught me things and helped me in my researches. I also gained much from time spent in study and practice at the Berkeley Dharmadhatu, founded by Chögyam Trungpa, Rinpoche, and from listening to several other Tibetan and American teachers, especially Dawa Norbu, of the California Institute of Asian Studies. My thanks to Paul Clemens and Nancy Mikuriya, Anatol Fetisoff, and Byron Pitts, for various contributions.

Contents

Contents

OPEN
SECRETS

1. East Is West, and West Is East

The first trucks rumbled over newly built highways in Tibet—a land where people had always traveled either on horseback or on foot—in the mid-1950s, the same years when the American public was just beginning to take an interest in Buddhism.

The systematic importation of the Industrial Revolution into the last outpost of ancient Oriental civilization had commenced in 1951, when Chinese troops established a garrison in Lhasa. Tibet's political status was unclear in those post–World War II years, and the Chinese sought to resolve the lack of clarity by establishing Tibet as a portion of the People's Republic of China. The highways were built to connect Tibet with China and facilitate the movement of troops within Tibet. While the Chinese constructed roads and airports and factories, they also took steps to reduce the power of the Buddhist leadership, and launched a propaganda campaign designed to reduce Buddhism's popularity with the Tibetan people. All these actions were part of the

1

same general project, which was to convert the ancient la-maist society into a modern Marxist one.

Meanwhile, in the land of superhighways and department stores, many people were searching for something else, some deeper knowledge that could be applied to their own lives. Some of them discovered Buddhism. The books of the Japanese scholar D. T. Suzuki and the English-turned-American theologian Alan Watts were first published in American editions in the 1950s and found a new readership beyond the small circle of scholars who studied Oriental religions. This was the first wave of what would eventually become a massive infusion of Eastern philosophy into American culture. It was a modest beginning: In the 1950s most people knew Buddhism only in its Japanese form, Zen, and even that was regarded by many people as a passing fad, the plaything of Beat poets, little more. The media lost interest in Zen toward the end of the 1950s, but many Americans—especially many young Americans—did not.

In Tibet the first decade of Chinese occupation ended with an armed rebellion. It was a valiant but awkward and ill-fated uprising by native guerillas who believed—with some encouragement from the American Central Intelligence Agency—that they could drive out the Chinese and establish an independent Tibetan state. The rebellion was never a serious threat to the Chinese, but it did bring about a change: Until then the Dalai Lama had been permitted to continue as the nominal ruler of Tibet. But in 1959, at the height of the rebellion, it appeared that the Chinese might be about to take the Dalai Lama prisoner. These vague fears were exacerbated by an ominous note from the Chinese commander in Lhasa, inviting the Dalai Lama to attend a theatrical performance at the Chinese garrison. It specified that he should come without his ministers or a bodyguard. Rumors circulated wildly about Lhasa, and Tibetan troops and civilians—some thirty thousand of them—surrounded the Norbu Lingka, the summer palace where the Dalai Lama was in residence. There followed a hectic week in which crowds of Tibetans remained encamped around the Norbu Lingka while both sides—the Dalai Lama and his advisers inside the palace, the Chinese about a mile away—tried to decide what to do next. On March 17 the Chinese began firing mortars into the grounds of the Norbu Lingka, not far from the palace itself, and the young ruler became convinced that his life was in danger. That night he and his immediate family were spirited out of the palace, and taken by horseback across the Indian border. After his escape the fighting intensified for a short time; before the Chinese had completely suppressed the rebellion, thousands more Tibetans had followed the Dalai Lama into exile. Among them were many Buddhist lamas, the country's most eminent intellectual and spiritual leaders.

So ended the closest thing to a theocracy left in the modern world, a civilization ruled by lamas and geared entirely toward the practice of Buddhism; and so began the great diaspora of Tibetan culture. Among the many young lamas who fled Tibet in 1959 were Tarthang Tulku, who was appointed to a teaching fellowship in Buddhist philosophy at Sanskrit University in Benares; and Chögyam Trungpa, who studied at Oxford University and established a Buddhist meditation center in Scotland.

In America, Zen mingled with other streams of change and became a part of what Theodore Roszak, looking for a phrase to describe the *Zeitgeist* of the 1960s, spoke of as a new "counter-culture."[1] Roszak identified among the mentors of this counter-culture Alan Watts and Beat-Zen poet Allen Ginsberg; he noted that in the political activism of the 1960s there was a strain of mysticism, of religiosity, quite different from anything that had been part of the radicalism of the 1930s. He was right, but he did not foresee that the activism of the 1960s would soon subside, whereas the mysticism would not.

Tibetan Buddhism reached the United States about ten years after the rebellion and the exodus of lamas from Tibet. Tarthang Tulku came to America in 1969 and founded a meditation center in Berkeley. In 1970 Chögyam Trungpa arrived; one center had already been started in Vermont by a group of his former students from Scotland, and later in 1970 another was founded in Colorado. Each of these became another connecting link between two of the world's most dissimilar civilizations: one that had been for centuries remotely and mysteriously Oriental, and one that had become the prime example of Western technology and materialism.

The Orient and the Occident had pursued separate courses of evolution for so long that they seemed to be distinct halves of the human race, as naturally differentiated as the two halves of the human brain: the East subtle and indirect in its ways, suspicious of machinery and change, attuned toward the cultivation of inner wisdom; the West brash and forthright, bent upon progress, inclined toward an objective mode of intelligence that equated data with knowledge. Two different worlds, which could not quite understand each other. "East is East and West is West," wrote Rudyard Kipling, "and never the twain shall meet." Until very recently, that stood unquestioned as the final statement on the subject.

Yet both East and West are changing rapidly, and borrowing much from each other. The Orient is assimilating Western technology, while the West is discovering the ancient Eastern methods of personal exploration. Hydrogen bombs explode in China and the smoke of automobile factories pollutes the air of Japan, while Americans take up meditation, practice yoga, and visit psychic healers. East is West and West is East. The text for the time is not Kipling's famous line but the prophecy of Padmasambhava, the eighth-century guru of Tibetan Buddhism: "When the iron bird flies, and horses run on wheels, the Tibetan people will be scattered like ants across the world, and the Dharma will come to the land of the Red Man."

Tibetan Buddhism has come to the West, and its arrival marks a new stage in the assimilation of Oriental thought into American culture, because although Tibet was determinedly backward in its *mechanical* technology, it was highly advanced in the kind of knowledge it considered important. It had for centuries made spiritual development its chief social priority, and it was the inheritor of some 2500 years of Buddhist theory and practice. Tibetan Buddhism—the body of teaching that came to India with the exiles and is now being disseminated in the United States—is probably the most complete system of Buddhism in the world.

BUDDHISM DATES BACK to approximately 528 B.C., the year in which, in a country already teeming with explorers of inner space, the young Indian nobleman who is now called the Buddha experienced enlightenment and began to teach his doctrine of the "middle way," freedom from extremes of self-indulgence and self-torture. His teachings included a set of concepts about how the mind works—the oldest psychology of which the world has any record—that became the basis of a sophisticated system of thought. Its main propositions were that ordinary human existence is an unsatisfactory state in which people make themselves miserable as a result of a basic misunderstanding of their own nature, and that there exists another state, *nirvana*, which is a release from this misery and a different way of being in the world. After the Buddha's death, nirvana began to achieve a status comparable to that of heaven in Christianity—the beyond, the inconceivable. The Buddha's followers strove to reach nirvana by achieving a status of perfect sainthood, and Buddhist philosophy began to take on some of the characteristics of what anybody would recognize today as established dogma—not one dogma but several, as Buddhists disputed fine points and separated into various schools clustered around this or that interpretation of the Buddha's teaching.

This continued over a period of some four hundred years, and then there emerged, perhaps around the time of Christ (the exact chronology of early Buddhism is much in doubt), a new and more liberal school of Buddhism that was not so impressed by the legendary virtues of the Buddhist saints. This new Buddhism tended to emphasize the principle of "Buddha-hood" over the historical Buddha, and it was also a more social path: People were encouraged to develop compassion and to think of themselves as involved in an evolutionary struggle involving all sentient beings. Compassion was held to be inseparable from enlightenment, and nirvana came to be thought of not as "out there" someplace, at the end of some rainbow, but as latently present in every moment of ordinary existence.

The proponents of the new Buddhism began to call the older tradition the "lesser vehicle" (*hinayana*) and their own approach the "greater vehicle" (*mahayana*). Both forms of Buddhism spread to other parts of the Orient: The conservators of the lesser vehicle moved southward into Ceylon and Burma, where it became (and still is) the major religion. The teachings of the greater vehicle traveled to Tibet and China and Japan.

Early in the fourth century a Tibetan king converted to Buddhism, thus beginning the 1600-year history of mahayana in Tibet. The mahayana sorted itself out into many separate schools. In China one school increasingly focused on meditation—called *djana* in Sanskrit—and became identified by a Chinese version of that word: *ch'an*. Transplanted again to Japan, Ch'an Buddhism became Zen Buddhism. Zen is a very pure form of mahayana Buddhism, with few remaining traces of the complex psychological concepts of the hinayana.

As Buddhism spread, the Tibetan monasteries became

centers of Buddhist scholarship. Information moves so easily in the modern world that we can scarcely comprehend the scope of this effort, the gigantic physical and intellectual energy that went into it. The Tibetans developed a written language, learned other languages, and collected and translated hundreds of works of Indian philosophers. Many long journeys were made, back and forth along the footpaths that wound through the world's highest mountains, as Tibetans traveled to India to study at its monasteries and Indian teachers came to Tibet.

The exportation of Buddhism from India was accompanied by its gradual disappearance from its country of origin. The decline of Indian Buddhism spanned a period of many centuries and was brought about by many forces, including the wars of Muslim conquest that resulted in the death of countless Buddhists and the destruction of centers of Buddhist culture.

But of course Buddhism lived on: Ceylon, Burma, and other countries of Southeast Asia preserved the hinayana; Japan and China practiced the mahayana; Tibetan Buddhism included both hinayana and mahayana, and also the mysterious "third force" called the *vajrayana*, or Tantric Buddhism. This is a part of Buddhism that—with its flavor of the occult and the erotic, its hints of shortcuts to enlightenment—many Westerners find especially intriguing, and are also especially likely to misunderstand.

The origins of tantrism are lost, and there is no consensus among Buddhist scholars as to where it came from and when it first became part of Buddhist belief and practice. It clearly involved absorption of teachings from non-Buddhist sources: the Hindu philosophers, the Indian yogis, and probably, at a later date, the Sufis, the holy men of Islam. Tantrism was a major force in Indian Buddhism by the seventh century, and Tibetans usually trace the history of the vajrayana in their country from the eighth century, when Padmasambhava came to Tibet from India and launched a great resurgence of activity that included the translation of many more texts into Tibetan.

The word *vajra* is sometimes translated as "lightning bolt," which conjures up images of great power, such as the psychic energy the yogis believe to be available within the human body, and also suggests an instantaneous burst of enlightenment: The vajrayana is sometimes called the "short path." But vajra also means "diamond," and the vajrayana is best translated as the "diamond vehicle." The diamond image is used in many ways in Tibetan Buddhist literature to describe the universe and the basic quality of mind—clear, brilliant, indestructible, many-faceted. Vajrayana teachings stress self-acceptance and self-study, and the naturalness of enlightenment.

The Tantric tradition is a heritage of texts—the tantras—and of practices: chants, body movements, rituals, images to be held in the mind as visual meditations. It is in a way the most elitist form of Buddhism, since much of its lore is kept secret and transmitted only to students who are judged ready to handle it. Even many of its written texts are in code, meant to be understood only by people who have already attained a certain level of knowledge or experience. But in another sense it is the most open and accessible of all forms of spiritual practice: It offers the beginner simple practices (such as chants) that are easy to learn and that "work" to bring people into higher states of consciousness without their having to be concerned about *why* they work. In fact, that concern can get in the way if it becomes too abstract and intellectual.

The vast storage of Tantric lore includes a practice in which sounds are employed as meditation devices, the student being given a specific mantra to use when initiated into the practice; this has already reached America by way of India, under the name of Transcendental Meditation, and has helped thousands of Americans. Another strain of Tantric teaching that may have relevance to the assimilation of Buddhism into American society holds that the monastic life is not necessarily the best path for the student of Buddhism to follow, and that it is perfectly permissible to live as a normal householder and enjoy the pleasures of the world. There are Tantric rituals involving sexual intercourse, and whether or not any of these ever make their way into the mainstream of American culture, the basic principle underlying them—the refusal to separate sexuality from spirituality—might help to heal our schizoid split between religious prudery and the Playboy ethic.

The vajrayana, which incorporates Tantric practices within a framework of Buddhist philosophy, may indeed be the "short path" to enlightenment. But it is not an easy path; its more advanced practices are both strenuous and dangerous, involving long hours of concentration and frightening journeys into the depths of the unconscious. It also requires a relentless honesty, a willingness to look oneself in the face, figuratively and, sometimes, literally: Six hours of sitting before a mirror is a highly recommended meditation exercise. But despite the extreme difficulty of some of its practices, the vajrayana has a universal message: Its insistence on valuing every experience and its attempt to unite spiritual growth with everyday life deserve attention from all of us.

Tibetan Buddhism, then, is a highly eclectic spiritual tradition. Some teachers say it should be studied in a sequence that recapitulates the history of Buddhism. Begin with the earliest teachings of the Buddha, proceed through the psychology of the hinayana, and come finally to the mahayana and vajrayana. In Tibet, formal training often followed this pattern: Monks would spend most of their lives studying the classical Buddhist scriptures, and would be introduced to the more esoteric practices only after years of preparation. Not many Americans are going at their studies that systematically, but some are investigating far enough to discover that Buddhism contains far more than they had previously suspected.

The arrival of Tibetan Buddhism in America began the second stage of the assimilation of Buddhism into our culture. The first stage began in the 1950s, with Zen. In a couple of decades—an instant in the history of Buddhism but a rather long time by our own speed-freak rate of calculating change—Zen made a comfortable home for itself. We can see its considerable literary impact in the works of poets such as Ginsberg and Gary Snyder, and trace its influence in major schools of psychotherapy, such as Gestalt, that have emerged here since the 1950s. The value of meditation is now generally recognized by scientists and the medical profession, and its practice is no longer confined to dedicated nonconformists. When it became known in the 1970s that Edmund G. Brown, Jr., candidate for the office of governor of California, was a meditator and a student of Zen, nobody became upset over it; it was weird, but not *too* weird. The Zen influence in American culture may turn out to be most conspicuous in the world of sport: Eugen Herrigel's *Zen in the Art of Archery*, published in the United States in 1953, introduced us to the idea that the balanced state of mind acquired in sedentary meditation could also be carried through into physical action, with a great achievement of precision and grace. Since then Americans have discovered the "inner" aspects of such pastimes as tennis, skiing, and running. There are probably more students of Zen on the tennis courts of America than there are in its meditation centers.

Zen is a good form of Buddhism to be exposed to first. It is simple and unpretentious and readily accessible. Since it avoids intellectualism, the newcomer to Zen is not required to plunge into the study of philosophy. Its literature—such as the aphorisms of Zen masters, the riddlelike *koans* used as teaching devices, the discourses of Western interpreters such as Watts—is poetic and readable. The practice of meditation is rewarding in itself, and easily sampled by anyone who has the patience. Zen is—or seems to be—fairly easily detached from the Japanese culture.

Even so, its modest cultural trappings have been a distraction for many people, in different ways: Some took a dislike to the ritualistic, specifically Japanese parts of it and consequently never managed to find out whether it held anything of use to them. Others became thoroughly enchanted with Oriental culture, and some even convinced themselves that they had to go to Japan in order to discover their true inner natures.

This problem—the problem of separating the universal human message from its cultural medium—becomes greater as we approach Tibetan Buddhism. Tibet is far more alien to us than Japan is. The United States and Japan have been closely involved with one another, for better or for worse, since Commodore Perry sailed into Tokyo harbor in 1853. But only a handful of Americans have ever visited Tibet, and very few know anything of its language, culture, or history. Some Japanese art, especially that influenced by Zen, is beguilingly simple and easily appreciated by the Western eye. Tibetan Buddhist art, is, to say the least, a bit bizarre: It goes in for frightful, grimacing deities who dance on human bodies and wave skulls and swords about, often with multiple sets of arms. Male figures are often shown in copulation with a female of the species who obligingly winds her body about his while he proceeds with his sword-brandishing. Everything Tibetan has an aura of the supernatural. It is hardly surprising that so many people find Tibetan Buddhism a completely alien matter, perhaps of interest to specialists or to restless seekers after the exotic, but hardly something to be of value to the everyday business of life in New Jersey or Idaho or Oregon.

Still, I will try to convince you that much of Tibetan Buddhism is sensible, practicable, and understandable. It includes some principles—ways of dealing with one's own experience, ways of looking at the world, ways of taking

The four-handed lord Mahakala, a protective deity.

care of oneself—that most of us can put to use. This knowledge will have to be teased apart from its cultural trappings
and domesticated.

Some people are taking up the study of Tibetan language, history, literature, and art in order to understand and
help preserve the heritage that has come to America with Tibetan Buddhism, from the scrolls and manuscripts that were
carried across the Himalayas on the backs of fleeing lamas.
But most of us, of course, will not have time for such studies
and will simply be interested in finding the parts of the tradition that we can use, that can do something about

the tension and meaninglessness and loneliness and confusion that are so much a part of daily existence in this marvelously clever country.

Tibetan Buddhism teaches that one must learn to experience the present as it is, free from rigid agendas, and accordingly the people who have brought it to the United States have no strong preconceptions about what kind of a place it will make for itself in our lives. They seem to regard the whole phenomenon as a highly interesting experiment.

Buddhism also teaches that everything changes and that it is futile to expect anything—your body, your state of consciousness, a relationship, the world—to be the same from one moment to the next. It seems hardly likely, in view of this, that anybody familiar with Buddhism would expect it simply to be transplanted from one place to another without changing greatly in the process. Religions spread by intermingling with the native religions and cultural traditions in each new area they come to. Christianity co-opted many items from pagan faiths as it moved about the world—consider the history of Christmas—and Buddhism also took on new forms in each society that adopted it. It merged with and changed old faiths and philosophies and social structures. It came across the mountains from India laden with an enormous psychological/philosophical system, which had been produced over centuries by India's best and most exquisitely nit-picking intellectuals, then arrived in China and made common cause with the cloudlike simplicity of Taoism. Moving on to Japan, Buddhism became the official faith of Samurai warriors. It is a remarkably protean body of ideas, yet its central core—made up of difficult propositions, such as the insistence that the self is an illusion—survived each move.

In Tibet, the religion that preceded Buddhism was Bön, a shamanic faith densely populated with spirits and local deities. Buddhism absorbed much of this: The story of Padmasambhava's life says that he encountered and tamed the spirits of the Tibetan mountains and made them protectors of the monasteries; the wrathful demons became part of the complex symbolism of the vajrayana, to be understood as projections of the unconscious. In the process Buddhism became different from what it had been in India; it developed a subtle and sophisticated view of the relationship between the mysterious cosmos and the equally mysterious human mind. As Buddhism became a bit like Bön, Bön slipped to the status of a minor religion. But it did not disappear entirely, and I am told by Tibetans that there were still-functioning Bön monasteries in the 1950s—yes, monasteries, because over the centuries Bön had become more and more like Buddhism.

Buddhism went through several stages during its long history in Tibet: New philosophical schools emerged; there were reformations and counterreformations. Buddhism changed, and so did the country. Tibet evolved from a warlike kingdom into a peaceful theocracy, ruled by the lamas. Since the events of 1959— the abortive revolution, the flight of the Dalai Lama—the Chinese have endeavored to convince the world that their coming helped the Tibetan people to rid themselves of a parasitic ruling class, the lamas. This may well be true, but it misses the point of what Tibetan civilization was about. It was a society mobilized around a certain goal, which was spiritual development; it was geared toward that purpose the way some societies are geared toward war and others are geared toward commerce. It had a structure and a set of roles reflecting that purpose. The lamas performed their duties, which were to study Buddhist philosophy and perform the Tantric meditations and rituals, and the people supported them. As far as I can tell, the average Tibetan did not think lamas ought to grow their own food, any more than the average American thinks an astronaut ought to make his own shoes.

I am not being facetious in making that particular comparison. The Tibetans believed that the lamas were exploring the universe, that what they did was work, and that it was worthwhile. We believe precisely the same thing of astronauts. The Tibetans made the lamas the rulers of the country. We elect astronauts to the United States Senate.

The Chinese characterize the lamas as a fat and lazy aristocracy, which is not quite accurate. Three years of solitary meditation in an eight-by-ten-foot cell—a required stage in the career of monks of the Kagyu school—is hardly the life of an idle hedonist.

The Chinese have overstated their case somewhat, as people with political axes to grind usually do. Conquest rarely proceeds without rationalization, and the fact is that the Chinese conquered Tibet, imported thousands of families to live there, and uprooted the civilization that had existed before they came. But there is nothing particularly novel about such an operation; the colonization of America followed the same agenda, and we are not in a comfortable position to assume an attitude of moral superiority toward the Chinese in this respect. All we can really do is recognize that one civilization came to an end, that much of its culture dispersed to other lands, and that it was replaced by new people with a new social structure. Everything changes. The official ideology in Tibet is now the one that Karl Marx developed to explain Europe's industrial revolution, and the cutting edge of Tibetan Buddhism is now to be found in such places as the Nyingma Institute in California and the Naropa Institute in Colorado.

This brings us to the intriguing question of what form Buddhism is likely to take in the United States, what native shamanism of our own it is likely to merge with. Obviously it is not likely to retain its purely Tibetan form, with monasteries in every city and a lama instead of a politician in the White House—although we could perhaps do worse—but it will probably have to find some more modest econiche for itself among our other ideas and institutions.

As it happens, we have any number of contemporary

social and intellectual movements that are marching in roughly the same direction as Tibetan Buddhism. It is amazing how closely this ancient religion parallels humanistic psychology in relation to such concepts as awareness, peak experiences, and self-actualization, and how the Nyingma relaxation system known as *kum nye* resembles the sensory-awakening and relaxation techniques of the human-potential movement.[2] Buddhist psychology has much in common with Western phenomenology and its introspective approach to the study of the human mind; in fact, Buddhist psychology, which we will look at in chapter 3, *is* a system of phenomenology. We will also see that there are points of contact between the vajrayana and existentialism, between Tantric symbolism and Jungian psychology, between Tibetan medicine and the emerging disciplines of holistic health, between Buddhist cosmology and the frontiers of modern theoretical physics, between Buddhist attitudes toward life and the values of the environmental movement. The most popular chapter in the late E. F. Schumacher's *Small Is Beautiful* was his discussion of "Buddhist economics," showing how Buddhist concepts such as right livelihood, the "middle way," and compassion for all beings could be carried into the world of work and business. Those ideas would not have touched off such a great response if there had not already been something stirring within many of us—a dissatisfaction with the dehumanizing and exploitative aspects of our usual economics—that made us ready to understand them and take them in.

We will be making a mistake if we try to persuade ourselves that Tibetan Buddhism is merely an Oriental form of phenomenology or humanistic psychology. It is a good deal more mysterious than that—perhaps not as mysterious as some of the legends about Tibet picture it to be, but nevertheless distinct in many ways from Western systems.

Tibetan Buddhism has a great tradition of esoteric lore, of knowledge kept secret from the general public and passed on from teacher to student. This is part of what has made Tibetan Buddhism the subject of so much fantastic speculation since it was first encountered by the Western world. The existence of an esoteric tradition in a religion implies that it functions on different levels of meaning—that it has outer forms, exoteric material for people who are not able or ready to take in its secret content, and inner meanings for those who have been initiated.

The exoteric material in a religion usually serves social or political purposes: It provides codes of morality to regulate behavior, rituals to sacralize the transitions of individual life and the events of the year, a common store of beliefs that help people sense their connectedness to one another and to their culture. The esoteric material is concerned with personal growth and the evolution of the mind.

It is the esoterica, of course, that gets most of the attention from people who are now taking an interest in Eastern religions. We seem to be experiencing a religious revival in which large numbers of people, impatient with the shalt-nots and one-day-a-week piety of the churches and synagogues, search for something more like what the old sorcercer Don Juan of the Carlos Castaneda books calls "a way with heart"—something that is truly mysterious, that awakens a sense of the grandeur of the cosmos and the deep commonality of the human species, that has its roots in the secret spaces of personal experience. So we turn to Sufism, the esoteric "heart of Islam"; to the Arica school and the Gurdjieff tradition, both closely connected to Sufism and also to the long-suppressed Gnostic esoterica of Christianity; to the Jewish esoterica of Hasidism and the cabala. Trying to pry open the secrets of our own all-too-familiar yet somehow elusively incomprehensible lives, we turn to the ancient teachings, prowl through the shadow world that, much to the dismay of religious power structures everywhere, can always be found somewhere behind the respectable but bland face of official religion.

Much of what was secret in Tibetan Buddhism is not secret anymore. Many of the guardians of its lore, concerned that it not be lost entirely, have permitted it to become public property. Mandalas and religious drawings that were once kept hidden in the monasteries and shown only to students who were considered ready to deal with them are now reproduced on high-speed presses and sold in print shops. Obscure Tantric rituals are described in minute detail in popular and scholarly books.[3] A considerable amount—but not all—of esoteric Tibetan Buddhism is now available to the West.

But with all this, the wall between the inner and outer dimensions of Tibetan Buddhism has not really crumbled. Esoteric material, however widely disseminated, remains secret until it is understood and experienced; in a way, the secrets are always safe. Their purpose is to help you discover your own nature, and therefore they have no meaning except insofar as they cause something to happen within your own consciousness. It is sometimes said of Zen that all of its knowledge is nothing more than a finger pointing the way. When the practices or insights of an esoteric tradition work, their effect is to bring about an expansion of personal awareness that is—contradictory as this may sound—spontaneous. And a piece of esoteric practice given to somebody who is not ready to use it can be useless. You can find in several places descriptions of highly advanced vajrayana meditations; they tell you how to visualize various symbols—deities, circles of lunar and solar light, colors, and so forth—how to expand them and contract them and hold them in various centers of your body, and none of it is of much use to a person who has not explored the subject of the symbolism and laid a foundation of simple meditation and visualization practice. You might as well hand an electric typewriter to a Tibetan yak herder.

The esoteric-exoteric distinction also involves morality. Every religion has its rules about how people are supposed to behave. Such codes of morality are usually exoteric, handed out as the word of God, meant to be obeyed (whether one understands their purpose or not) because they make the society work. In the esoteric traditions, codes of morality are less important for the simple reason that the ultimate purpose of the spiritual effort is to attain a level of personal development at which morality is natural. It is discovered within oneself, and external authority is no longer necessary or meaningful. This principle is not foreign to Western psychology. Lawrence Kohlberg theorized that the most highly developed human beings operate out of inner moral principle.[4] The same point is made by Abraham Maslow in his studies of healthy, "self-actualizing" people, who, he says, have relatively little respect for the formal rules and regulations of the society but at the same time a strong sense of concern for others.[5]

Tibetan Buddhism is a self-development technology of a most curious kind: It refuses to tolerate any belief that a "self," in our usual meaning of the word, really exists. That is, there is no permanent or *a priori* definition of who and what you are. The process of development that it asks you to undertake is one in which you will be continually prepared to let go of your preconceptions of what you are and should become.

Tibetan Buddhism can be thought of from a personal-development perspective, as a way of achieving harmony in one's individual life, or it can just as easily be looked at from a cosmic or evolutionary perspective, as one aspect of nature's effort to produce a higher order of beings. This may seem at first to be an either-or proposition, but eventually it turns out not to be contradictory at all. One of the basic principles of Buddhist philosophy is *samanvaya*, the act of reconciling contradictory ideas by carrying them to a level of understanding at which it can be seen that they are not really contradictory. The mark of success in personal development, from the Buddhist perspective, is a transformation of your own ideas of what you are. Such a transformation inevitably involves a reexamination of ideas about the nature of your relationship to external reality, to other people, and ultimately to the cosmos.

Basically, Tibetan Buddhism is a technology, not a mechanical system for changing the physical environment—which is what we usually think of when we talk of technology—but a self-development system. It is a technology in the sense Lewis Mumford had in mind when he urged us to take a wider and more organic view of human progress:

> Tool-technics, in fact, is but a fragment of biotechnics: man's total equipment for life. . . . I submit that at every stage man's inventions and transformations were less for the purpose of increasing the food supply or controlling nature than for utilizing his own immense organic resources and expressing his latent potentialities, in order to fulfill more adequately his superorganic demands and aspirations. . . . To consider man, then, as primarily a tool-using animal, is to overlook the main chapters of human history. . . . Man is pre-eminently a mind-making, self-mastering and self-designing animal; and the primary locus of all his activities lies first in his own organism, and in the social organization through which it finds fuller expression.[6]

In Mumford's view one of the great early technological accomplishments was the development of speech: the long, slow cooperative effort by which people learned to use the organs of eating and breathing for new purposes that expanded the possibilities of life—in fact, transformed the human species so that it was quite different from what it had been before. No external tools were used in this enterprise, which very closely resembles the Tibetan Buddhist effort to find new ways of using the mental and physical equipment we all possess. If we think of technology in the way Mumford suggests, as the expression of our "mind-making, self-mastering and self-designing nature," then systems for the development of consciousness are obviously technology.

Mumford's perspective is not easy to grasp; his is a dissenting voice, not quite in harmony with the usual arguments about technology, either pro or con. But the effort is worthwhile. It gives us a much better approach to Tibetan Buddhism than our rather puzzled and cliché-ridden notions about the East and its religions.

Then, instead of seeing the West as technologically progressive and the East as technologically primitive, we can see them as alternate paths of development—the West concentrated on the "outer" technology of tools and machines for altering and developing the environment, the East concentrated on the "inner" technology of practices for altering and developing the human organism. Each became somewhat overspecialized, and is now compensating by absorbing a bit of the other kind of technology.

Understanding that Tibetan Buddhism is a technology does not make it any less mysterious, but it does give us a better picture of the nature of the mystery. In one of the Buddhist scriptures, Gautama tells his followers that he has held back no teaching from them, concealed nothing in his closed fist. Although some of the lore is strange to Western ways of thinking, and although teachers are sometimes reluctant to impart material until they are sure the student is prepared to deal with it, the content of Tibetan Buddhism is accessible. Its secrets are not really "out there" any more than enlightenment is "out there." The key to its esoterica is the recognition that a large part of yourself is secret from yourself—available, yet blocked by such obstacles as fear, ignorance, the ego, and socially conditioned beliefs about human nature.

2. Buddhist Basics

Although I have referred to Tibetan Buddhism as a religion, and will again from time to time, what needs to be understood is that it is not a religion in the customary Western sense of that word. It is not about God; it is nontheistic. Tibetan Buddhist writings do not explicitly attack the belief in a creator or prime mover of the universe; they simply don't raise the subject. They are in pursuit of another kind of truth. Buddhist thought is opposed to reification, to turning processes into things and events into objects. This applies to turning creation into a Creator. The Buddhist position seems to be that whether you spend your time worshiping God or arguing that He doesn't exist, you are wasting a lot of energy on something that is unknowable, and being distracted from the equally awesome—but accessible—mysteries of your own life.

So let us, for the moment, put aside the idea of God. Although Tibetan Buddhism does involve deities and cosmic ideas that are close to what Westerners generally mean by

God, the concepts are not the same. Concepts are not "things" at all, in fact; Tibetan thinking is wary of turning forces into objects.

It seems to me that the most basic premise of Tibetan Buddhism is that there are Buddhas. This idea starts us out on a somewhat different approach from that of religions such as Christianity and Islam, which assert that there is a God, and that there is also a specific human being who stands in a special relation to Him. Since Buddhism does not have a God, it cannot have somebody who is regarded as God's prophet or messiah. The significance of the historical figure known as Lord Gautama, the Buddha, lies elsewhere; this becomes especially clear when we note that for the Tibetans, "Buddha" is a generic term, applied to a whole class of people, and not merely another name for Lord Gautama.

The word *buddha* comes from the Sanskrit root *budh*, meaning "to know" or "to wake up." The Tibetan term for a Buddha is *sang-yas*, which communicates two meanings: a clearing-up of mental impediments, and an expansion of qualities. These terms indicate that a Buddha is somebody who knows something or is aware of something, and that the awareness has brought a personal development or growth.

The historical Buddha, Gautama, is, for the Tibetans, not a solitary messiah but an evolutionary principle, an exemplar of what it is possible for human beings to become. Buddhahood is described as a natural state, a way that all humans are capable of being. The Tantric writings say that Buddhahood is not so much something to be attained as to be discovered, simply *looked at* and integrated into one's view of the world.

This does not mean that the Buddhist texts, Tantric or otherwise, ever suggest that Buddhahood or enlightenment comes easily; however readily available it may be, the obstacles are formidable. Consider a fly circling about in a stuffy, spray-laden room. Although there is a certain amount of poison floating in the air and it is not a particularly satis-

factory place, the fly doesn't leave the room. Why not? A
door is open, and all he would have to do is head in its direction. Yet he continues to circle about. It is a short distance
to the door and the fresh air, and his optical equipment is capable of perceiving the exit, but he doesn't go that way.
From the point of view of an intelligent and compassionate
human being who observes the fly's behavior it would seem
that it would be the easiest thing in the world for the fly to
go through the door. In a way it *is* easy, and in a way it isn't;
it depends on your point of view.

This metaphor is not quite fair to the Tibetan view of
Buddhahood, because it represents the enlightened state as
being "somewhere else" and not immediately present in
everyday experience. But it does express the idea that Buddhahood is not something supernatural or beyond reach.
"Everything is Buddha without exception," writes Saraha.

Among the foundation stones of all schools of Buddhism is the set of precepts called the "four noble truths,"
which, according to tradition, were the content of the first
sutra, or sermon, the first discussion that Gautama had with
a small group of friends and followers after he had attained
enlightenment. The truths are summed up in four Sanskrit
words: *dukkha, samudaya, nirodha, marga*. The word *dukkha*
means "dissatisfaction"; the message of the first truth is that
life is full of dissatisfaction. *Samudaya* means "cause" or
"origin"; the second truth is that there is a source of the dissatisfaction. *Nirodha* means "extinction"; hence, the source
of irritation can be removed. The final truth is contained in
the word *marga*, or "path," implying that there is a way.

The Buddha's actual words on the subject of the truth
of "unsatisfactoriness," as recorded in the first sutra, were
hardly in themselves enough to serve as the foundation for a
great religion: He mentioned the facts of sickness and death,
of grief and sorrow, of the presence of things we dislike and
the absence of things we like—nothing that has escaped the
attention of the Western world. We have also, I would say,

come to similar conclusions regarding the second truth: that there is a cause to the suffering, and that the cause is related to the abnormal human capacity for craving, greed, desire. Niccolò Machiavelli came very close to the first two noble truths in a passage in his *Discourses:*

> When men are no longer obliged to fight from necessity, they fight from ambition, which passion is so powerful in the hearts of men that it never leaves them, no matter to what heights they may rise. The reason of this is that nature has created men so that they desire everything, but are unable to attain it; desire being thus always greater than the faculty of acquiring, discontent with what they have and dissatisfaction with themselves result from it. . . .[1]

The Buddha's discussion moves beyond familiar Western concepts with the third truth, nirodha: the extinction of suffering. In the Christian tradition the extinction of worldly suffering is death, one hopes with a rebirth in heaven; for people who are not too strongly connected to the faith, the preferred remedy is to get or do something that will make you feel good: Eat a meal, become rich and famous, take a vacation, take a pill. Another way we commonly deal with suffering is to slip into a state of seminumbness, to sleepwalk through life and abandon hope of any richer experience. The Buddhist message is that there is a way out of existential unsatisfactoriness that involves neither death nor acquisition nor withdrawal but rather an alteration of your way of being in the world. The fourth truth is marga, the path, and that, of course, is what all of institutionalized Buddhist practice is about. The Buddha himself did not go on at great length about it. He gave some information about what the path is not, and some information about what it is.

First, what it isn't: Buddhism is not, despite its many pronouncements against greed, a religion of self-debasement. The India of Gautama's time was populated with holy men who demonstrated their holiness through various forms of what Christianity calls "mortification of the flesh"—and the Buddha said that wasn't it. Such practices were, he said, "painful, unworthy, and unprofitable." On the other hand, outright hedonism, utter devotion to the pleasures of the senses, was also not the way. The path he offered was the "middle way," between those extremes.

That brings us to what the path is. It is sometimes described as the "eightfold path," because the Buddha mentioned eight elements, eight areas of life that need to be done "right" in order to break through the pattern of suffering: view, aim, speech, action, livelihood, effort, mindfulness, and concentration.

"Right view" means adopting an attitude in which you are prepared to accept tentatively and to test out the four noble truths. You are not asked to accept them on faith; perhaps the greatest difference between Buddhism and Christianity is that Buddhism very explicitly *does not* require an act of faith. In one of the sutras the Buddha says:

> Do not put faith in traditions, even though they have been accepted for long generations and in many countries. Do not believe a thing because many repeat it. Do not accept a thing on the authority of one or another of the Sages of old, nor on the ground that a statement is found in the books. Never believe anything because probability is in its favor. Do not believe in that which you have yourselves imagined, thinking that a god has inspired it. Believe nothing merely on the authority of your teachers or of the priests. After examination, believe that which you have tested for yourselves and found reasonable, which is in conformity with your well-being and that of others.[2]

The elements of aim, speech, action, livelihood, and effort outline a down-to-earth code of ethics in which the seeker is counseled to avoid stealing, killing, lying, improper sexual conduct, and destructive occupations. These precepts are handed down not as God-given commandments for behavior but rather as a set of guidelines for living in a way that is likely to be of value to yourself and to others, to lead you in the right direction.

I find it interesting that the part of the eightfold path that has become best known in America is the concept of "right livelihood." It has become something of a catchphrase recently; more and more Americans seem to have become concerned that so many of the available ways to earn a living are either unproductive or actually destructive, to the society, to the environment, to the future, to other people, or to themselves. The phrase from the sutra has become widely identified with the urge toward more useful and harmonious occupations.

The other part of the eightfold path that is already familiar to us, although it goes by different names, is mindfulness. The Western version of this is Gestalt therapy, the awareness path to mental health. I don't mean that Gestalt therapy is the same as Buddhist mindfulness practice— we will see in the next chapter that there are fundamental differences—but there are some strong similarities that give us an entrée into this important part of Buddhist doctrine.

One similarity between Tibetan Buddhism and Gestalt therapy is the emphasis on the *how* of life rather than the *why*. Gestalt therapy, unlike Freudian psychoanalysis, works with the here and now and does not take the patient off on a long voyage through the past in search of the roots of present behavior. In Buddhist texts Gautama frequently advises his followers to give up seeking explanations of how things got to be the way they are, and to concentrate instead on the business at hand. There is a favorite passage of mine in one of the sutras, wherein the Buddha is engaged in a long dialogue with a holy man named Potthapada. First Potthapada asks if consciousness is different from the soul. The Buddha has no answer. Potthapada then asks, "Is the world eternal? Is this alone the truth and any other view mere folly?"

"That, Potthapada," replies the Buddha, "is a view on which I have expressed no opinion."

Potthapada proceeds to fire more questions:

"Is the world not eternal?"

"Is the world finite?"

"Is the world infinite?"

"Is the soul the same as the body?"

"Is the soul one thing and the body another?"

"Does one who has gained the truth live again after death?"

"Does he not live again after death?"

"Does he both live again and not live again after death?"

"Does he neither live again nor not live again after death?"

To each one of these questions the Buddha replied, "That, too, Potthapada, is a matter on which I have expressed no opinion." Asked why, the Buddha said, "This question is not calculated to profit; it is not concerned with the Dharma; it does not redound even to the elements of right conduct, nor to detachment, nor to purification from lusts, nor to quietude, nor to tranquilization of heart, nor to real knowledge, nor to the insight of the higher stages of the Path, nor to Nirvana. Therefore it is that I express no opinion about it." Asked what he does express an opinion about, the Buddha goes back to the basics: dukkha, samudaya, nirodha, marga.[3] All this sounds remarkably like an exchange between a Gestalt therapist and a head-tripping client.

The other point of similarity between Gestalt therapy and the Buddhist path is the great stress on awareness/mindfulness. In Gestalt therapy the goal is improved psychological health; the Gestaltists insist that we can hold on to our neurotic hangups only if we successfully keep ourselves *un*aware of what we are really doing and how we really feel: To become aware is to change. Hence the so-called "paradoxical theory of change," as one Gestalt therapist formulated it:

> *Change occurs when one becomes what he is, not when he tries to become what he is not.* Change does not take place through a coercive attempt by the individual or by another person to change him, but it does take place if one takes the time and effort to be what he is—to be fully invested in his current positions. By rejecting the role of change agent, we make meaningful and orderly change possible.[4]

Two of the elements in the eightfold path concern awareness: right mindfulness and right concentration. Mindfulness has to do with a constant attentiveness to what is going on in the mind and body; concentration (samadhi) is the one-pointed state of mind achieved in meditation.

The objective of Buddhist practice is the extinction of the *samsaric*, "ego-centered," state of mind that leads one into suffering; this state of mind is described by such words as "craving," "passion," "attachment," but the Buddha does not ask us to repress our feelings, any more than the Gestaltists ask us to change through inner or outer coercion. Both say the problem is in being out of touch: Pay attention, perceive the truth, and you become free. "Distortion and dispersion, the causes of passion, must be replaced by incisive attentiveness," writes the nineteenth-century Tibetan lama Mi-pham. "Practice of watchful examining, like a light in darkness, destroys the last vestige of injurious passion."[5]

The practice of mindfulness is so important in the Tibetan tradition that the four noble truths begin to take on a distinctly Gestalt-like cast, which makes them considerably more accessible to the American mentality. When I studied them under an American teacher in a class on Tibetan Buddhism, they had been Occidentalized into four "generally valid observations": One, life is full of discomfort and suffering. Two, the discomfort has a pattern, a cause; it is not merely random. Three, to the extent that one investigates the patterning, there can be a radical change in it. Four, there is a way that this can be done.

Although there are similarities between Gestalt therapy and Buddhist mindfulness practice, there is also a gaping difference in their basic assumptions. Gestalt therapy was influenced by the philosophy of holism and by Gestalt *psychology*, which had to do with the brain's ability to organize scattered perceptual data into units (*Gestalten*). Frederick Perls, the originator of Gestalt therapy, had been particularly influenced by the work of Gestalt psychologist Kurt Goldstein, who worked with brain-damaged soldiers and studied the capacity of seriously maimed human beings to organize themselves and function. Under Goldstein, Perls said, he first began to think of the human organism as a whole and not as a bunch of characteristics.

Buddhism says that the human being is a bunch of characteristics—not characteristics, even, because that has a sense of stability; more a flow of events. The human reality at any time is merely a collection of *dharmas*, various mental processes that are usually organized under five basic headings: feelings, perceptions, impulses, consciousness, form. The only whole Buddhism recognizes is the whole of the cosmos, or, perhaps, the totality of your experience at a given moment, so long as the experience is not blinkered down by some concept of a continuing self that is doing the experiencing.

This idea, which is the most radical part of Buddhism, and also the very heart of it, arose in opposition to the Hindu concept of the *atman*, the indestructible personal soul that was held to be the core of human existence. Buddhism says: *anatman*, no *atman*, no soul, no discoverable "I," no self.

This appears to be a strange metaphysical proposition, as abstract as any of the questions of Potthapada. But the

Buddhists insist that it is the simple observable truth of human experience, that a systematic paying of attention to your own life—mindfulness and concentration—will lead you to make that discovery. They defy you to discover anything else. "Quick," says the Zen master in the famous koan, "show me the true self that was yours before your mother and father were born."

The Buddhists also say that this is not a negative or nihilistic idea but a positive discovery of the way things are. One exposition of Buddhist thought says:

> According to the Buddha's teaching, it is as wrong to hold the opinion "I have no self" (which is the annihilationist theory) as to hold the opinion "I have self" (which is the eternalist theory), because both are fetters, both arising out of the false idea "I AM." The correct position with regard to the question of Anatman is not to take hold of any opinions or views, but to try to see things objectively as they are without mental projections, to see that what we call "I," or "being," is only a combination of physical and mental aggregates, which are working together interdependently in a flux of momentary change within the law of cause and effect, and that there is nothing permanent, everlasting, unchanging and eternal in the whole of existence. . . .[6]

This idea runs straight through the 2500-year history of Buddhism, from its earliest teachings through all its migrations and cultural transformations.

As a philosophical idea *anatman* has fascinated people for centuries, during which time it has been heatedly debated and widely misunderstood. But Buddhism is not just a philosophical system. Its challenge is neither to prove nor disprove the concept at the intellectual level but to experience it, to awaken to that reality. The correct perception of the nature of one's own experience is held to dissolve the pattern of craving and dissatisfaction. The release is attained not by forcefully suppressing desire but by getting a clear look at precisely who it is who desires precisely what. There are, of course, real needs that should be met, but there are countless other experiences of desire that are merely the confused cravings of a cluster of events that thinks it is somebody.

There is no permanent self in Buddhism. In fact, nothing is permanent. Everything changes. The Buddha's last words were a reminder that all things are perishable, that anything that comes together can also come apart. The individual consciousness mirrors a cosmos ever in flux, its elements continually combining and recombining into new patterns. Whatever you are at the moment, or think you are, is one of the patterns. Alexandra David-Neel gives this Tibetan parable of the workings of the human personality:

A "person" resembles an assembly composed of a number of members. In this assembly discussion never ceases. Now and again one of the members rises, makes a speech, and suggests an action; his colleagues approve, and it is decided that what he has proposed shall be executed. Or now several members of the assembly rise at the same time and propose different things, and each of them, for private reasons, supports his own proposal. It may happen that these differences of opinion, and the passion which each of the orators bring into the debate, will provoke a quarrel, even a violent quarrel in the assembly. Fellow-members may even come to blows.

It also happens that some members of the assembly leave it of their own accord; others are gradually pushed out, and others again are expelled by force, by their colleagues. All of this time newcomers introduce themselves into the assembly, either by gently sidling in or by forcing the doors.

Again, one notes that certain members of the assembly are slowly perishing; their voices become feeble, and finally they are no longer heard. Others, on the contrary, who were weak and timid, become stronger and bolder; they become

violent, shouting their proposals; they terrify their colleagues, and dominate them, and end by making themselves
dictators.

The members of this assembly are the physical and
mental elements which constitute the "person"; they are our
instincts, our tendencies, our ideas, our beliefs, our desires,
etc. Through the causes which engendered it, each of them is
the descendant and heir of many lines of causes, of many series of phenomena, going far back into the past, and whose
traces are lost in the shadowy depths of eternity.[7]

The principle that gives coherence to this flux over time
is *karma*, meaning "action" or "cause and effect": One situation, or combination of events, gives rise to another situation
or combination of events.

This is a vastly impersonal and matter-of-fact business,
as Buddhism sees it. It is the source of Buddhist morality,
but it is not moral in the sense that God has ordained that
some things are sinful and others virtuous; the principle
simply states that whatever situation you are in now is the
result of other events, and that whatever you do will have
consequences. There is no particular time limit on this: Your
personal situation can be seen from a great evolutionary
height as the product of everything that has happened in the
cosmos since the Big Bang, and the results of your actions
will echo down through the millennia.

Karma includes everything that we call "heredity"—all
of genetic evolution—and also environment. The social context in which we live is the product of karma, and so is the
individual consciousness. Indeed, the samsaric mind itself—
the belief in a separate ego—is itself an effect of social
karma. Several Western schools of psychology and sociol-
ogy have also come to the conclusion that the self is the
product of society, that the "I" of each of us is the result of
interaction with parents, peers, culture. Social values and
beliefs are "internalized," so that they become a part of us.
Social karma conditions our innermost thoughts. Let us take

a look at how two Western writers—both talking about Buddhism—present this. First, Erich Fromm:

> Every society, by its own practice of living and by the mode of relatedness, of feeling, and perceiving, develops a system of categories which determines the forms of awareness. This system works, as it were, like a *socially conditioned filter*; experience cannot enter awareness unless it can penetrate the filter.[8]

And, Nolan Jacobson:

> The result of this canalization is that a style of life is trapped in the brains of those who enact it. . . . It is covertly embedded in the attitudes with which life is regarded and in the habits in which children are reared. It links individuals into families and communal forms of life. It cleaves indestructibly to every member of a social order, so that none can take a detached view in order to introduce radical social departures, precisely because the person or group wishing to change the prevailing order is itself the living embodiment of it. . . .[9]

Literally, *samsara* means "going around in circles"; the mind goes around within the narrow confines of social reality, stuck in socially programmed habits and behavior patterns and ways of thinking; the waking-up process called "enlightenment" is a breakthrough to a fresher appreciation of reality, less fettered by social values and beliefs.

This gives us a new insight into the morality of Buddhism. The sutras are not heavily moralistic. The instructions about the eightfold path give some suggestions about what you should and should not do, but they are presented as guidelines toward enlightenment. It is easy to see why so many people have described Buddhism as an unusually practical kind of religion. "Transcendental pragmatism," Aldous Huxley called it.

The monastic life, which countless Buddhists have chosen, is a path of renunciation: celibate, vegetarian in most countries, Spartan, plain. The Buddhist monk is required to live under conditions considerably more severe than those imposed on the general public, because this is believed to be the most efficient way to become enlightened, to break free of attachment and the narrow world view of the unenlightened, samsaric mind. The monk's behavior should be above ordinary morality. Other Buddhists, the wild outcasts of tantrism, have sometimes taken precisely the opposite path: to live below the level of ordinary social morality, thus to become free of lust through satisfying it, to steer clear of the subtle egoism of being more virtuous than other people. Still other Buddhists have chosen to live just like other people, to get married and obey the laws and make no effort to be different in any way. The only element these life-styles have in common is that they take ordinary social morality to be nothing more than a reference point, never an ultimate code of behavior. The question, in choosing a way of behaving, is, What works best?

Buddhist morality is often associated with a simple doctrine of reincarnation and a moral-retribution approach to karma; that is, there is a "you" that is born again and again in various forms; if you do something evil in your present existence, there will be undesirable consequences for you in a future one, and vice versa. This concept of reincarnation did not originate with Buddhism, but was part of the culture of India, where Buddhism came into being; it was simply the accepted reality for most people, and for many it still is. So, although Gautama did not talk about reincarnation, as we see from the Potthapada Sutra, Buddhism was naturally placed within that context.

I have heard some Tibetan Buddhists speak as if the doctrine of reincarnation were literal truth, and I have heard others advise their students not to take it too seriously. It is an exoteric doctrine; thus, it is all right to believe in it—perhaps it is even valid—but it is also a symbol or echo of a more subtle and complex esoteric teaching.

The simple idea of reincarnation does not square with the anatman doctrine: If there is no real ego, no soul, then there can be no transmigration of it from one life to another. In a sense—and this is the easiest part of the esoteric view of reincarnation—many people are "reincarnated" in each of us, given seats in the assembly that we call the individual mind. In Buddhism, which does not make a strong distinction between objective and subjective reality, the various people who occupy your consciousness—Socrates, Shakespeare, Karl Marx, whoever—are "real." And each of them was once also a crowd, a karmic cluster of influences from the past and from the social context in which they lived.

There is a "supernatural" side to the esoteric view of reincarnation. It is generally accepted, as in the Tibetan Book of the Dead,* that some portion of the individual consciousness may survive after death. This is not precisely "you," but rather a surge of energy from your consciousness that churns on, like the undigested cud of a cow, after the body has died.

It is also commonly accepted that there may be a continuity from one human being to another, when there is a task that cannot be completed in a single lifetime. This does not, however, quite come up to the popular Tibetan folk belief that the soul of a lama, upon his death, automatically proceeds to be reborn in the person of some child who is then sought out and hailed as the lama's successor. The lamas may indeed believe there is a certain transmission of energy in such cases, but this belief is not strongly connected to any concept of an individual ego. In Buddhism a person who occupies a role *is* in many ways the same as a previous occupant of the role; there is no specific identity that can be separated from the social role.

* The Tibetan Book of the Dead, a document crucial to Buddhist teachings, is discussed further in chapter 8.

The esoteric view of reincarnation is much grander than the simple exoteric belief, and at least as mysterious. It sees the individual consciousness as connected in many ways to other individual consciousnesses, past and present, much as each strand of a spider web connects to all the other strands. Some of these connections are well within the Western ideas of reality, and others extend into what we would call the supernatural. It does not rule out the possibility of people's "remembering" past lives, as some people are convinced they have done. It suggests only that if you think you remember some past life that was "yours," you are still fixed upon an erroneous sense of ego.[10]

TWO OTHER basic concepts that are necessary for a nodding acquaintance with Buddhism are *karuna* (compassion) and *shunyata* (usually translated as "emptiness"). These concepts are closely identified with the mahayana, and are also strong currents in Tibetan Buddhism. They are both fairly straightforward notions, and yet, like so many ideas in Buddhism, they are capable of opening up new levels of meaning just when you think you have got them all figured out.

In the older, hinayana form of Buddhism the role model for the religious seeker was the *arhant*, the saint who had triumphed over desire through virtue and willpower. One of the marks of the mahayana is the charge that the arhant ideal, although admirable, is lacking in social responsibility. Some of the arguments surrounding the emergence of mahayana Buddhism sound remarkably like the contemporary American dialogues about the latent narcissism of the human-potential movement, its alleged preoccupation with the self-actualization of a privileged few and lack of concern for the progress of the society or species as a whole. In mahayana Buddhism the arhant ideal lost some of its status and was replaced by the *bodhisattva*, a being of great compassion who reaches the point of complete nirvana but chooses to live in the ordinary world among ordinary people, working for the enlightenment of others. The bodhisattva ideal is expressed in the Buddhist vow to work for the enlightenment of all sentient beings. This vow, renewed daily in many schools and monasteries, might sound a touch grandiose, but it is a healthy reminder that Buddhism offers no permanent resting place, no point at which you may proclaim that you have arrived at enlightenment.

It would be easy to get the impression that *karuna* has the role in Buddhism of a central moral principle, a way that people ought to try to be. That is true, in a way, but Buddhism is, as I have mentioned, not simply a system of morality; it is a statement about the human mind and a system for organizing the human consciousness. It says that when the nature of human experience is accurately perceived, one enters into an enlightened state of being: In that state, compassion is naturally present; it is as inherent to the enlightened or buddha mind as the condition of craving and dissatisfaction is to the samsaric mind. And since the enlightened state is held to be always latently present in ordinary experience, it follows that the feeling of compassion is also latently present; it is not something outside yourself that you should acquire in order to be a good person but something there, yet not quite noticed. Western psychology talks about repression and offers ways to rediscover repressed feelings, especially those involving sex and aggression. Buddhism suggests that our natural feelings of compassion and love are repressed as well.

Compassion is usually linked with a concept described by the Sanskrit word *shunyata*. This is one of the most slippery concepts in Buddhism. The Sanskrit word *shunya* means "empty," and so for decades most translators have told us that the Buddhists cultivate a mental state of emptiness. Since empty-headedness is not too highly valued in the West, other translators have hedged on this and suggested that perhaps *shunyata* deals with an experience of "voidness," or "nothingness." Whichever way you translate it, the word seems to suggest that Buddhism is a religion of total withdrawal from all conscious experience—a hard notion to reconcile with that of enlightenment, or "waking up."

H. V. Guenther, with the help of a couple of hyphens, offers a way out of this confusion; he suggests that the word *shunyata* might most accurately be translated as "no-thing-ness."[11] That is, the awareness that the Buddhist path seeks to cultivate is one in which perception and experience are quite rich and "event-full," but devoid of permanent and separable entities. Every "thing" is only an event in the flux that instantly gives way to another event; we are led into a cosmos that is all verbs, no nouns.

Experiencing *shunyata*—discovering that thoughts are not things—sets one naturally on the path toward enlightenment, say the Tibetan teachings, and is more effective than wrestling with any of the specific "problems" that your thoughts may present to you.

> By a doctrine which is similar to the application of fat to a wound when an arrow piece remains inside, nothing can be reached; by a doctrine which is similar to tracing the footsteps of a thief to a monastery when he has escaped to the forest and mountains, nothing can be gained, (but) *having declared one's own mind to be non-substantial* by its nature, the fetters of the world will fall off by themselves, because all is sunyata.[12]

Shunyata is closely related to the basic ideas of egolessness and impermanence. *Shunyata* and *karuna* are important and interrelated, said to combine into a state of supreme awareness, a state that is free from conceptions of permanent objects: That is how the state *thinks.* How it *feels* is described by *karuna:* It feels compassion and love. It is typical of Tibetan Buddhism to connect an intellectual proposition with an emotion. This connection violates the hardheaded idea that a concept is supposed to be merely *understood*, logically and dispassionately, and it offers a rich and warmly human way of experiencing the truth.

These are a few of the basic—very basic—ideas of Buddhism. Some of the concepts discussed—the four noble truths, the eightfold path, the concepts of nonself and the dissolution of all entities—are generally accepted by all Buddhists. The concepts of karma and reincarnation belong to a cultural world view that extends beyond Buddhism; they are taken literally by some Buddhists and not by others. The concept of enlightenment is the keystone of all Buddhist thought, and yet it changes, or seems to change, at different times and places. In some writings it appears to be a superhuman condition; in others it is very human indeed.

One of the worst features of Buddhism, in my opinion—and I am talking now about Buddhism in the United States, about its impact on Americans who come in contact with it—is that it permits people to erect an ideal of enlightenment as some way we ought to be, something we ought to go out and get in order to be better. It is something else to fret after and feel inadequate for not having. The ideal assumes a natural place in our pantheon of objects to covet, along with the perfect orgasm, the dream house, and the Academy Award. Even Zen, which is for the most part a wholesome addition to our culture, does far too little to free people from this unfortunate fixation.

The trouble is, as soon as you start developing a fixation on how you ought to be, you lose touch with how you are, and the essence of the Buddhist path is to be aware of how you are.

I find that the Tibetan Buddhist teachings, especially those given on a person-to-person basis, stay very close to this idea. The word *nirvana* is rarely used, except in reference to the older Buddhist texts. The most common Tibetan term for enlightenment is *tharpa*, which means "liberation."

Enlightenment is freedom from binding mental constructions, and that includes binding mental constructions about
enlightenment.

There is an old saying that "You can't get there from
here." The Buddhist message is rather different: "You can't
get there from *there.*" You can't get to enlightenment from
concepts about enlightenment. You *can* get there from here,
from your present experience. And as you penetrate more
deeply into Tibetan Buddhism, you begin to hear it telling
you that where you get from here is *here.* It turns out that
that fly circling in the stuffy room was outside all the time—
that fly, spray, room, observer, all were tricks played upon a
more expansive reality, and that the trick player is itself
samsara, the suffering consciousness.

So the Tibetan teachings tend to discourage grandiose
ideas of what it is like to become enlightened. Generally
they counsel you to follow the basic outlines of the eightfold
path, to live a reasonably sane and moderate life, whatever
that may be for you, and to try to stay awake and pay attention to what is going on in it. Observe your everyday experience (some methods for doing that are presented in
following chapters) and, if it appeals to you, watch your
mind in silent meditation.

Buddhism is not absolutely wedded to meditation.
Saraha, in his poems, jeers at yogis with their gaze fixed on
the ends of their noses, and ridicules the idea that you can
find something by meditating if it's already in your mind
anyway. Meditation is only a tool, but it is one that most Tibetan teachers use in many ways.

In its simplest form meditation is simply a calming of
the mind. It is—to return to the other metaphor we used,
that of the mind as a clamoring assembly—a way of letting
the voices die down a bit, to pay attention to the silence. In
that silence you may discover a truth that, although inex-
pressible in words, is very near the heart's deepest desire.

3. Your Mind: Now You See It, Now You Don't

Buddhism is complex and many-sided. Its lore includes rituals and codes of morality, written teachings, and esoteric practices passed on orally from master to student. It is richly ornamented with painting, sculpture, and architecture—everything from the austere ink-brush drawings of Japan to the gilded pagodas of Thailand and the mind-boggling symbolism of Tibetan tapestries and statues. Buddhism has produced, over the centuries, many schools and sects, and as it passed through the traditions of several different lands, it picked up along the way an enormous cultural superstructure. You could spend a lifetime in Buddhist scholarship, prowling through its caves and passageways, without ever absorbing more than a fragment of the whole. Yet at the core of it is something clear, simple, and accessible. If you begin at that core, whatever else you may choose to do (or not do) in relation to Buddhism will have integrity and purpose.

Buddhism deals with your experience. I do not mean

someone's concept of experience; I mean what is going on in you now, in your mind and body. That is the center of Buddhism, the home to which any study of it must always return. The Buddhist path is essentially a matter of dealing with your own minute-to-minute, everyday awareness. Keep that in mind, and you will not get lost amid the complexities.

As a "psychology" Buddhism is somewhat different from what most of us mean by that word: It is not for the purpose of studying the minds of other people, as is the case with most Western psychologies. Behaviorist psychology, especially, is a monument to our alienation from inner experience. It focuses on externalities, on measurable behavior, and considers nothing real or true unless it can be verified by someone else's research. Buddhist psychology is precisely the opposite: Everything has to be verified by your own experience.

The purpose of Buddhist psychology is to enable you to find out what is going on in your own mind.

This may sound rather strange at first. You are, after all, the possessor of your own mind; it has been with you always, and you undoubtedly assume that you are aware of your own thoughts. That assumption may be quite wrong, however: You may discover, if you employ some of the techniques of Buddhist psychology, that your ongoing conscious flow of thoughts and sense perceptions and emotions—everything that had seemed most ordinary and familiar to you—is a strange and uncharted territory that you have never systematically explored. In fact, you may discover that you have never really paid much attention to it, even when—perhaps especially when—you were most actively involved in "thinking."

Try asking yourself some questions about thinking, questions of the sort that a Tibetan teacher might use in a talk about Buddhist psychology: How long does a thought last? How many thoughts do you have in a minute? In a day?

Can you stop thinking? How do you feel when you are not thinking? Is there a different quality to different intervals between thoughts, or are such intervals always the same? How long can you pay attention to a single object?

And some questions about emotional states: How long does a feeling last? When you feel an emotion, where do you feel it? Do certain emotions come in groups or sequences? Which ones? Can you describe how you feel when you are happy?

These questions may seem childishly simple, even pointless. They will probably seem less so if you make a serious attempt to answer them. It is also likely that you will resist attempting to answer them. This is natural; the mind lusts after the great abstraction, the mighty insight, the next moment, the vivid memory of the past—anything but the homely reality of the present. We believe devoutly that life is something other than what is happening now, and we will search anywhere but right in front of our open eyes for its mystery.

Buddhism holds that the mystery—not only the central problem of life but also its solution—does lie right before us all, that it is open and accessible. If it is invisible, it is not because it is hidden but rather because we have systematically blinded ourselves to it. What we need to do is learn how to see. This can be stated, in a more Western manner, as a hypothesis: Close observation of your own mental processes is a powerful tool of personal growth. It can lead toward the resolution of personal problems, and also toward a fundamental shift in your sense of who you are, what you need, and how you relate to the world.

Let us consider further the resemblance between Buddhism and Gestalt therapy. The basic ideas of Gestalt are that the states we think of as mental illness (or neurosis, or simple immaturity) have to do with being out of touch with oneself; that recovery of awareness is the way to grow and become healthy; and that as we try to do this, our own minds sabotage the effort in many ways, throw up road-blocks in front of the truth. We should not be surprised by this similarity between an Eastern religion and a Western school of therapy; if a set of ideas has any validity, it will naturally surface at different times and in different places.

These Gestalt ideas are compatible with Buddhist teaching. However, Gestalt is strongly biased toward sensory experience and nonintellectual modes of self-discovery. Fritz Perls's famous call to "lose your mind and come to your senses" made a deep impression on his followers, and consequently Gestalt therapy has tended to take the "touchy-feely" route and to avoid the "head trip" to awareness. Buddhism is often believed by Westerners to be equally anti-intellectual, which is a misconception. It might be true of Zen, but it is certainly not true of the total Buddhist tradition, which includes the dharmas, a sophisticated system of introspective psychology. Tibetan Buddhism, standing by with the full tool kit, invites the student to use noncognitive practices such as chanting and body work, and also to study the mind with the mind, to think hard about thought.

THE DHARMA SYSTEM

The early Buddhists developed a phenomenology, a set of concepts about thought, to be used in self-exploration. Their effort, preserved in the writings called the Abhidharma, was a gigantic cooperative venture that occupied India's most creative and brilliant minds over a period of several centuries. It was as ambitious and vast, in its way, as our own Manhattan project or space program. It produced a set of descriptions of basic mental events, dharmas, that were believed to be the fundamental elements of existence.

The list of dharmas includes relatively simple items such as sense perceptions and emotions, and also complex mental processes, trance states, and enlightenment experiences. It is a kind of psychological atomic table. The dharmas, although capable of being identified and categorized, are never thought of as static entities; existence is conceived of as a flow of perceptions and emotions and mental activities that continually recombine.

The system of dharmas begins, simply enough, with the elements of sense perception: first the five organs of perception, and then the corresponding items—sounds, visual forms, etc.—that can be perceived by each organ. There is also a place for "elements with no manifestation," to account for our ability to experience sense perceptions when there are no corresponding external stimuli, as in memory and imagination. Closely related to the sense perceptions is the dharma called *manas*, which refers to the purely mental operation of processing sense data.

This sensory-data-processing operation, in the Buddhist view, goes on at an extremely high rate of speed: In fractions of a second, the mind leaps from one item to another, noting each sense perception separately. If you think you are tasting a piece of food and looking at a person and remembering something at the same time, what is actually happening is that your attention is flickering back and forth from taste perception to sight perception to memory perception, and also jumping to other sense data that momentarily arise in consciousness. You have an incalculably small instant of taste, instants of seeing your dinner companion, instants of paying attention to how your body feels, what you smell, things you hear, other images and sounds that arise in your mind.

The flow of consciousness, then, is not so much like a stream as it is like a motion picture, in which a series of still images appear to be a single moving image, or like the pointillist paintings of Seurat, in which many tiny dots are seen as a unified picture. The mind never stays long with the motion picture, it rarely looks at the whole painting, yet it is continually creating for itself continuities and wholes. If you can grasp the importance of the here-and-now perspective to the Buddhist psychology of perceptions, you are less likely to have trouble with Buddhist ideas about the self. The essence of this perspective is that your mind repeatedly constructs new versions of reality based on *ideas* of lasting images, but the ideas themselves rarely last very long. They are continually being revised, as the present, the past, and the future are continually being re-created.

Before we move on, try this: Pay attention to your own sense perceptions, and see if you can refute the Buddhist concept of sensory experience. Can you concentrate on a visual image and feel something with your hand at precisely the same time? Can you, then, also be aware of a remembered sound at precisely the same time you are experiencing the visual image and the touch perception? If you can't, can you become aware of how your mind shifts from one item to another? This effort is worthwhile simply for the purpose of developing your ability to experience sense data. If you are going to spend your life in pursuit of certain tastes and sights and textures, it makes sense to have a clear understanding of how the objects you associate with them actually taste, look, and feel. If you deeply explore any sensory experience—such as the taste of a rich dessert—you may find that you appreciate it more fully, or you may find that it is something you can do without. You may, in fact, find both.

Buddhist psychology identifies a number of "mental events" that may be present in any thought pattern. Keep it in mind, as we proceed to look at some of these parts of the dharma system, that they are better thought of as verbs than as nouns; they are not "things" but rather forces of mental functioning. Five of these mental events are said to be at work in every thought. They are called in Sanskrit *sarva-tranga*, which means, literally, "going everywhere." In English they are commonly described as omnipresent mental events. These five omnipresent mental events are called *sparsa, vedana, samjna, cetana,* and *manaskara.*

1. Sparsa

Sparsa, usually listed first among these five basic mental forces, translates as "rapport" or "contact." It relates to the principle, familiar in Western ideas about perception, that it is not strictly the sense organ that perceives an external object but rather the portion of the brain that processes that organ's activities. Seeing, for example, is done by the visual cortex as well as the eyes. In Abhidharma writings, sparsa is frequently defined as having three elements: the object, the sense organ, and the mind. All of this undoubtedly sounds familiar enough, perhaps even simplistic: The peculiarly Buddhist twist to it is the proposition that this object/sense organ/mind interaction is your real experience. Neither the external object nor the perceiving "you" is, in itself, capable of being experienced. When this proposition is understood—and the only way to understand it is to test it repeatedly—it leads toward a transformation of consciousness in which the familiar subject-object distinction disappears.

2. Vedana

The establishment of rapport gives rise to the dharma called *vedana,* or "feeling-tone." Every sensory experience is accompanied by a feeling-tone—positive, negative, or neutral.

> What is feeling? It is three ways of experiencing—pleasantly, unpleasantly, and indifferently. "Pleasant" is that which one would like to feel again (when the original feeling is over). "Unpleasant" is what one would like to get rid of when it is present. "Indifferent" is where neither of these two desires occur [*sic*].[1]

To experience this, try following your attention as it moves to different sense perceptions, and identify each as pleasant, unpleasant, or indifferent. Since this dharma also functions in relation to mental events, try closing your eyes and letting different memories, images, thoughts, pass through your mind while again you identify your response to each as pleasant, unpleasant, or indifferent.

The feeling-tone is an inner emotional experience that may or may not result in an action that can be seen by another person or measured by any device. An excellent summary by a Westerner of this process can be found in Jung's *Psychological Types.* Jung describes feeling as

> a kind of judgment, differing from intellectual judgment in that its aim is not to establish conceptual relations but to set up a subjective criterion of acceptance or rejection. Valuation by feeling extends to *every* context of consciousness, of whatever kind it may be. When the intensity of feeling increases, it turns into an *affect* . . . a feeling-state accompanied by marked physical innervations.[2]

3. Samjna

Another omnipresent mental process is the activity of classifying and defining events and objects, making sense out of the raw data of experience. It is called *samjna,* and can operate in different degrees of complexity. If you look out of an airplane window toward the ground, you might identify the color green, recognize a mass of green as a forest, and, if you have the information available, classify the forest as a number of giant redwoods within a national park in the state of California. The main characteristic of samjna, says one Abhidharma text, "is to know by association." It is a function, obviously, that develops and changes as we grow older and take in more information upon which to base our conceptualizations.

Samjna is also closely identified with the ego and with

the effects of socialization. There usually lurks about the edges of any concept a sense of who is doing the conceptualizing, and different societies have different ways of thinking. If your society does not teach you a word for an object or an experience, you may be barely conscious of its existence. Also, you may become so firmly sold on the official definition of what something "really is" that you lose your ability to perceive it freshly in the moment of experience. You look at a living plant, your mind classifies it as a weed, you experience a negative or indifferent feeling-tone in relation to it, and in the process you save yourself the trouble of paying any real attention to the perceptual richness of it or to the mystery of its existence. This danger, this latent deadness, is inherent in the conceptualizing act, and yet the process is a necessary part of dealing with the world.

Carlos Castaneda's old warrior Don Juan seems to be talking about the same mental process when he describes the *tonal*, the "organizer of the world" whose heroic task is to set the chaos of the world in order. Don Juan also warns that the *tonal*, although it protects our very being, has a tendency to turn from a broad-minded guardian into a petty and despotic guard.

The eighteenth-century Tibetan text called *The Necklace of Clear Understanding* says that conceptualization can be whatever you make of it: limited to concerns of pleasure and conventional ideas, expanded to a more aesthetic or philosophical frame of reference, or, wider yet, "wide and open like the infinite sky."[3]

This dharma, like the feeling-tone process, can best be ferreted out experientially: Try following your mind as it fastens on objects, and note the concepts that fall into place around the matters of which you become conscious. See if you can develop any sense of different degrees of complexity in your thoughts. One example would be to move from the relatively simple identification of an object's color on to more complex concepts. Try the same experiment with something "unreal," some random image that arises in your mind. Or try looking at a person; note how you name and define that person, then drop the name or definition and try experiencing the same person some other way.

4. Cetana

In the process of performing the above experiment, moving deliberately from one perceptual experience to another, you have been employing another omnipresent mental process called *cetana* and usually defined as "volition." This means not only the volition to act but, prior to action, the drive to organize the mental processes around a given object. The Buddhist psychological system is an active, dynamic one; it does not consider people to be simply passive processors of sense data.

By giving the concept of cetana a place in the category of omnipresent mental activities, the Buddhists were saying that when your mind settles on an object of attention and thought, it is an *act* on your part. You have made a decision, however tenuous it may be, and there is a reason for your decision. This is why some scholars prefer to translate the word as "motive" or "drive," to place further emphasis on the idea that when you choose to pay attention to something—to look at it, become aware of a feeling-tone response to it, conceptualize it—this is not simply a knee jerk of the mind but an action that relates to some sense of *purpose*. The purpose can be anything from a highly conceptualized and disciplined program of action to a simple craving for excitement. The latter tends to predominate. The cetana force, for most of us, is out of control—you can hardly be expected to control something you have never noticed—and lurches drunkenly from one object to the next. This is what the Buddhists mean by the "monkey mind," restless and random in its constant motions.

In some of the more positive descriptions of the cetana

force the Buddhist writers liken it to the head carpenter who starts the work off, or the military commander who wades into the fray with his soldiers behind him. These similes describe a mental energy whose function is to fasten on to an object and mobilize other mental energies.

To isolate the cetana function, put yourself into a state of concentration (or meditation) and observe the familiar problem of being distracted. The mind is drawn first to this idea, then to this or that memory or irrelevant thought; sights and sounds intrude upon your consciousness, seemingly of their own will. But to the Buddhists this is the play of your own power of mental volition. You are distracting yourself.

5. Manaskara

As a kind of countervailing force to this tendency, the mind also possesses a force called *manaskara*, which is translated by such words and phrases as "attention," "fixing in mind," "concentration," and "application." Attention is a very important function in Buddhist psychology, and the dharma system makes subtle distinctions among the several forces involved in the process of paying attention, different states of consciousness in which attention is the key factor. Two other dharmas involving attention are samadhi, the absorbed fixing of the mind on a single object of thought, and prajna, the ability to achieve a clear and precise awareness of any situation. Neither of these, however, is included among the omnipresent mental functions, and even manaskara, the most primitive form of attention, is absent from that category in many Abhidharma texts. The reason is that Buddhist psychology is most reluctant to recognize attention as a continuous mental process; it is more inclined to think of the various types of attention as events that happen only occasionally, and as powers to be cultivated deliberately.

Prajna became one of the most highly respected virtues in the Buddhist value system, second only to compassion. It is one of the dharmas, but it has a special place in the system: It is, so to speak, the dharma whose function is to observe and comprehend other dharmas in action. It is not always described precisely the same way: The more austere schools of Buddhism tend to stress its discriminative nature; prajna, they say, is the ability to be aware of precisely what you are experiencing, to know exactly what sense perceptions are functioning at each moment, what objects you are in touch with, what is the emotional quality and meaning of the experience, where it came from and where it is going. In other writings prajna takes on a slightly different nature and is seen as an appreciative awareness. When it is highly developed, you are capable not only of being clear about the nature of your experience but also of enjoying its unique and transitory character. Thus it partakes of both precision and celebration.

The word *samadhi* is frequently—and correctly—used to describe a state of deep meditation, but a state in which this kind of energy is activated can also be one of full yet relaxed concentration on an object of attention. It is the state of artistic creation, of productive work, of the best moments of athletic activity. It is the experience of being lost in what you are doing, so that the distinction between it and you seems to disappear. We have all been lucky enough to experience moments of samadhi, and a good way to develop a feel for the Buddhist perspective on attention is to consider the difference between a moment of effortless samadhi and the other kind of attention we are all familiar with, when the mind forces itself at gunpoint to stay with the task at hand. The essence of a true samadhi situation, you may notice, is that in such a state all five of the omnipresent mental processes are operating in harmony: There is (1) contact or rapport with what you are doing, (2) positive feeling-tone in

relation to it, (3) a clear conceptualization of it, (4) an attraction toward it that has a sense of purpose, and (5) an ability
to keep the attention fixed on it.

Intellectual development within the framework of Buddhist psychology is very heavily oriented toward learning
how to overcome the "monkey-mind" tendencies that are
present in all of us, and so characteristic of the unexamined
life. Buddhists sometimes liken the human condition to the
plight of a man lost in the desert: He wanders this way and
that, pursuing fantasies and images, forming and abandon-
ing one plan of action after another, and all the time going in
circles. One way to deal with such a situation is to throw
yourself on the mercy of a guide, if you can find one. Another way is to learn the territory, to become a crafty traveler who has carefully studied the desert and also has
trained the senses to be attuned to the minute signs and
events that are not noticed by the confused wanderer.

All of this applies, of course, to the everyday business
of life and not only to the search for enlightenment. You
can, if you wish, look at Buddhism from the Dale Carnegie
perspective and see it as a system for developing the intellectual clarity and strength of purpose that will enable you
to succeed, make money, become famous, or whatever it is
you want to do in the world. The older Buddhist traditions
would disapprove of this; the Tantric tradition would not.
The Tantric value system, which informs Tibetan Buddhism, calls a strength a strength. Regardless of what you
might have in mind when you develop it, it can be mobilized
toward the higher goal. The same powers of mind that effectively serve the purpose of the self-image can be used to
transcend it.

The dharma system was developed for the purpose of
freeing the human mind from the ego. The whole system,
with all its precise and subtly shaded terminology of mental
events, is a trap set to catch the ego, to show that when the
workings of the mind are rigorously investigated, a perma-

nent self is nowhere to be found. There is only movement, the ever-changing patterns of mental events, the flow of dharmas.

The dharmas are, then, a psychological system, and more than that. They are the keystone of the Buddhist view of the universe. They are as central to Buddhism as the concept of God is central to Islam, Judaism, and Christianity. The world view that the dharmas represent is one of tremendous immediacy; every phenomenon, every moment, is seen as a unique combination of mental events, elements that will never again come together in precisely the same way. This is true of the world as you experience it, and also of yourself. From this perspective, who you are becomes much less important than what you are and how you are right now. Ego language is replaced by dharma language.

Although the development of the dharma system was a heroic effort to free the human mind from its own manacles, the early spokesmen for what became mahayana Buddhism believed that the dharmas, too, set limits on experience. The hinayanists had revealed the ego to be an illusion; the mahayanists went a step further and declared the dharmas also to be an illusion, another attempt to grasp the ungraspable. The dharmas were modified by the concept of shunyata; all was declared to be empty, unknowable, ineffable, mysterious.

This was expressed in one of the classic mahayana scriptures, the Prajna-paramita-hridaya (heart of great wisdom) Sutra, which says, ". . . form is emptiness, and the very emptiness is form; emptiness does not differ from form, nor does form differ from emptiness; whatever is form, that is emptiness, whatever is emptiness, that is form. The same is true of feelings, perceptions, impulses and consciousness. . . . All dharmas are marked with emptiness, they are neither produced nor stopped, neither defiled nor immaculate, neither deficient nor complete."[4]

Although some mahayana schools, notably Zen, no

longer use the dharma system of self-analysis, it remained an important part of mainstream Buddhism in India and is still a highly valued element in the Tibetan technology of personal development. The dharma system lost status as the irreducible and absolute reality of the universe, but was retained as a tool of self-exploration.

This may be hard for Westerners to understand, but it is typical of Buddhist thought to be more concerned about an idea's usefulness than about its claim to be absolute truth. Since all truths are manifestations of mind, the way to judge any concept is by its value to a given mind at a given level of development. You use the dharmas like a ladder in order to get to a place from which you can throw away the ladder, and perhaps even see that it was not absolutely necessary to begin with.

This is probably the best way for us to approach the Abhidharma teachings—to regard them as something useful rather than to embrace them as ultimate truth. They are a rigorous and intelligent description of mental functioning, meant to be used in a sustained effort of self-study, self-psychoanalysis.

This has the sound of psychotherapy, and a careful inventory of the content of one's conscious mind certainly has that kind of applicability and value. There is no discernible boundary line between therapy and religion in Buddhist thought; the effort to overcome one's emotional difficulties is also the spiritual path; health is the precondition to enlightenment.

The therapeutic power of a developed capacity for self-observation lies in the fact that many emotional problems are actually deliberate misrepresentations of one's own experience. In our desperate struggle to survive and be happy we experience a pleasant event vividly, once, and then try again and again to assemble just exactly the right combination of conditions that will make that situation come again, but it never does, and while we pursue that rigid but illusory idea we lose touch with the reality of present experience. Just as the ego futilely attempts to tie a rope around the wind, to make fixed and permanent what is by nature always changing, so do our emotional miseries attempt to rigidify our experience into safe programs. The mind becomes like the demented computer, Hal, in the film *2001: A Space Odyssey*, which began to sabotage the great cosmic mission for which it was created.

If you can learn to watch the mind at work and *see* those fixed concepts of who you are, what you must do to be happy, how things must be, what awful event might occur if you act a certain way, then you can evaluate your insights against your real experience. And what you will often find is that many of these insights are merely illusions, wispy fantasies with no roots in your present felt experience. With every such discovery the doors of perception are cleansed and you awaken to a fresh sense of the rich and flowing present.

I know an American psychologist who has developed the simple exercise of adding the phrase "up to now" to any statement having to do with who you are, what kind of a person you are, what you believe, what you like or dislike, and what you can't do. The exercise does not demand that you reject any part of yourself, or consciously change, but only that you regroup yourself around your present experience; it is a trick for catching your self-concepts in the light, where you can get a look at them.

Many Westerners seem to think that Buddhism is based on a belief that the ego is evil and must be overcome. This is not quite the case. Buddhism is based on the belief that the ego is an illusion, a lie we tell ourselves, and that the truth can be discovered. It does not demand that you renounce all worldly happiness but rather counsels you to pay close attention to how you make yourself unhappy. It tells you that your main problem is a case of mistaken identity: You go through life clinging to a cheap, twisted, and obsolete concept of what you are, when you are in fact something grand and infinite and mysterious. This ego illusion is powerful, but vulnerable; it does not thrive under the glare of self-investigation, where it can be seen.

The actual practice of self-exploration can be carried out either in meditation or in ordinary, everyday activity. Meditation—sitting still, quieting the mind, observing it— provides a certain concentration and freedom from outer distraction. You will find, soon enough, that there are plenty of distractions anyway. The practice is not as easy as it sounds. If you attempt to fix your mind on anything, you will find your attention repeatedly wandering, but you will learn to bring it back gently again and again. If you try to observe your thought, you start out thinking of yourself as the observer, and then you float away; you *are* the thought, and the observer is lost.

I once heard a Buddhist teacher compare the mind to a flock of birds. This is a good example of the dharma view of thought: a flock of birds that moves as a unit, darting this way and that, continually changing its shape and direction. He sketched out this image and then expanded it to include a person who stands on the ground and observes the flock in flight. What happens when you begin the work of self-observation is that your consciousness shifts back and forth: Sometimes you see your mind, sometimes you don't. Sometimes you are the observer, and sometimes you are the flock of birds. The goal is to learn to be both at the same time. This is the cultivation of prajna, of what is sometimes called the "power of simultaneous awareness."

The dharma system is a kit of tools for self-exploration. We have handled some of the tools here and will look at some more of them when we deal with emotions and higher states of consciousness. I am not at all convinced that the entire dharma system will survive the move to Western culture; undoubtedly it will change. What is happening now is that many students are exploring the system and adapting parts of it. Some are learning Sanskrit and Tibetan in order to be able to get more deeply into the meanings of the various terms.

To use the dharma system effectively you should embark on a program of action that combines self-study with study of the system. There are some dangers involved here, because some parts of the system are difficult to understand, and the books that attempt to present it to English-speaking readers do a lot of bickering about how various terms should be translated. You can easily get confused and fail to learn how to make the system work for yourself. The way to avoid this is to stay close to your own experience. The dharma system was developed by people whose raw material was their own experience; out of centuries of inner search and cooperative work and debate, it was shaped into something that was believed to be generally valid for the human mind. It became a common vocabulary for self-exploration.

Anthropologists tell us that societies develop vocabularies for objects and events that are important to them. The Trobriand islanders have an exquisitely rich repertoire of words for the yam, reflecting all its growth stages and uses; the Eskimos have many words for snow. In attempting to translate the Eskimo vocabulary into English we get backed into strange corners and improvise word combinations such as "cold snow," "bluish-white snow," "wet snow," etc. These are approximations of the original meanings. To get at those meanings, one could work hard on the definitions, take part in the translators' debates, and worry terribly about what the Eskimos had in mind. But the only way to discover the real meaning would be to go out and look carefully at some snow.

4. Vajrayana: The Diamond Vehicle

The vajrayana, the major force in Tibet's religious history, is Tantric Buddhism. This takes a bit of explaining: Tantrism is an ancient, broad, and diversified religious movement that has both Hindu and Buddhist forms, and is in some respects separate from (if not disowned by) organized religions. Not all tantrism, in short, is Buddhist. Buddhism is also an ancient, broad, and diversified religious movement, and not all Buddhism is Tantric; Tantric practices and ideas are vigorously rejected in the hinayana schools, and not much admired by mahayanists either. But most Tantric Buddhists hold other forms of Buddhism in great respect; the vajrayana reinterprets some aspects of the hinayana and mahayana, but does not reject much outright. The Tibetans, especially, seem always to have been an eclectic people who made it a point to explore every possible corner of Buddhism. Thus, their monasteries acquired enormous libraries, with material from all schools of Buddhist philosophy.

Many Tibetan monks, as I have mentioned, were in-
structed to emphasize the classical studies in their early
years, and only progressed into the Tantric lore in later
adulthood, presumably when they were less likely to be
corrupted by it. There were also monks who, judged unsuit-
able for a lifetime in scholarship, were encouraged to choose
life careers as artists, or as musicians or dancers in Tantric
ritual. And there were also lay Tantric practitioners who
married and worked at ordinary jobs, found time when they
could for study and meditation, and employed Tantric rituals of sexual intercourse. Tantrism, in a rather moderate
form, pervaded Tibetan culture.

In many other parts of the Orient the Tantric tradition
acquired a rather seamy reputation. There is a tenth-century
Indian drama, the *Rajasekhara*, in which a Tantric hero sings
his song of the spiritual life:

> As for scripture and spell, they can all go to hell
> My teacher excused me from practicing trance
> With drink and with women we fare mighty well
> As so on to salvation we happily dance
> I've laid a young wench on the altar with me
> Good meat I consume and I guzzle strong drink
> I've a fur for my bed, and I get it all free
> What better religion could anyone think?[1]

In its most extreme form, usually associated with certain cults in Bengal, tantrism taught deliberate violation of
all rules of society and spiritual practice. The seeker should
try every sensation, commit any crime. The schism between
the exoteric and the esoteric becomes a complete break; all
that is outwardly respectable is scorned. All the no-no's of
traditional spirituality—sex, alcohol, meat eating, material
prosperity—are praised. Although this brand of tantrism is
definitely on the outer limits of the movement and is certainly not the mainstream of Tibetan Buddhism, it is true

that there are—as the West is now discovering—Tantric rituals of sexual intercourse.

Ritualized sex—involving breathing exercises, meditation, and the prolonged sexual contact known as *maithuna*—
is well known in the Orient and has been practiced for centuries. It is not, as Westerners sometimes take it to be, all
there is to tantrism, but it is an important part of the tradition in both its Hindu and Buddhist branches. Tantrism is a
spiritual movement that has always taken sex seriously, integrated it deeply into its view of the universe.

Western religions have their erotic symbolism also, of
course, but in nothing quite like the explicit forms it takes in
Tantric art, where deities and great religious teachers are
frequently depicted in the act of copulation. In some paintings the guru sits cross-legged in meditation with the female
partner sitting on his lap and facing him, her arms and legs
wrapped about his body. These drawings can be interpreted
in different ways: as literal illustrations of a Tantric sexual
ritual, or as a statement that the fully enlightened human is a
male and female being, a unification of sexual energies.

The subject of sex, like all else in tantrism, can be approached at many levels. You can begin with the proposition
that all parts of life are sacred and that a profound experience of erotic love opens the mind to a sense of awe and
wonder akin to religious experience. Another approach, in
the context of mainstream Buddhist philosophy, is based on
the often-reported experience of a loss of the usual sense of
self in intercourse, a transcending of boundaries so that the
partners are experienced as one. There is also the idea that
the way to become free of a binding passion—in this case,
sexual lust—is to go into the act that is desired rather than to
retreat from it. One of the Tantric texts states:

> Just as water that has entered the ear may be removed by
> water and just as a thorn may be removed by a thorn, so
> those who know how, remove passion by means of passion

itself. Just as a washerman removes the grime from a garment by means of grime, so the wise man renders himself free of impurity by means of impurity itself.[2]

All of these ideas are valid parts of the Tantric tradition, but the most important part of its sexual philosophy is the concept of essential male and female energies. This pervades the Eastern world view and takes many forms: The same polarities can be stated as active and passive, positive and negative, lunar and solar. The idea of equating one sex with action and the other with passivity sometimes raises protest among Americans opposed to sexual stereotyping, but if it is any consolation, the two wings of Tantric tradition are diametrically opposed on the question of which is which: Among the Hindu Tantrics, the dynamic principle is equated with the female and the static with the male; among the Buddhists, it is the other way around. The static energy corresponds to such essentially inward properties as wisdom and realization, whereas the dynamic side relates to outgoing aspects such as compassion and strength. The symbolism also relates the dynamic energy to cognitive or discursive knowledge, the static to the more symbolic or intuitive aspects of understanding, thereby coming close to the relatively recent scientific discovery of the differences between the right and left hemispheres of the brain. However the polarities may be described, the essential idea is that a synthesis of them is the highest goal of Tantric practice.

It is axiomatic to Buddhist thinking, and indeed to Eastern philosophy generally, that everything contains its opposite; the male and female forces are *both* present in every human being. Some Tibetan Buddhist teachers insist that the actual union of man and woman in sexual intercourse is not necessary for the union of the two energies; that in Tantric art the copulation is merely symbolic, that the goal can and should be achieved through solitary yogic practices. So, although there is a basic theme to be found in tantrism, there is great variety in how it is interpreted and carried into practice. Some Tantric paths can take you into ritualized sex, and others into chastity and meditation; they all head toward the same goal.

The Tantric tradition is also criticized for its close relationship to occultism. You will find in tantrism almost everything that is connected with the popular Western conceptions of magic: secret teachings, scriptures in code, the practice of drawing symbols on the ground and uttering spells to call up deities, supernatural powers that can be used for good or evil.

I doubt that contemporary Americans can comprehend what a blow it was to some of the European—particularly British—intellectuals who studied Buddhism in the late nineteenth and early twentieth centuries when they followed its historical development and found what it had come to. Here was Buddhism—a sublime teaching, which seemed to them nothing more than a rational and highly ethical way of dealing with the hard realities of human life—turning toward libertinism and superstition. The emergence of the vajrayana, which to Tibetans is an evolutionary progression to higher levels, appeared to some Europeans to be a degeneration. There are still scholars who have the utmost respect for the early Buddhist works, the sutras and the Abhidharma, but who regard the mahayana as a decline into sentimental mysticism and the vajrayana as an utter capitulation of the Buddha's noble teachings to the more corrupt strains of Indian spiritualism and Tibetan shamanism.

I don't propose to enter that argument here—feel free to make your peace with any part of Buddhism that appeals to you, or with none at all—but I would like to communicate a more complete image of what the Tantric tradition and the vajrayana mean in Tibetan Buddhism.

Tibetans translate the Sanskrit word *tantra* as *gyud,*

which means a kind of thread. The symbolism of thread, of weaving, turns up again and again in the Eastern spiritual disciplines. In the Muslim world weaving is a form of spiritual practice, and among the Sufis, rugs are recognized as precious expressions of inner wisdom. The weaving of thread is a metaphor for the deep interconnectedness of all life in a bewilderingly multifaceted cosmos. A German scholar of Buddhism, Helmuth von Glasenapp, summed this up well. He wrote:

> The notion that the whole universe with the totality of its phenomena forms one single whole, in which even the smallest element has an effect upon the largest, because secret threads connect the smallest item with the eternal ground of the world, this is the proper foundation of all tantric philosophy.[3]

Tantric philosophy blends with and illuminates the basic ideas of Buddhism—nonself, samsara/nirvana, liberation through awareness—and carries them into more complex realms of symbolism and psychophysical technology.

A human being in the Tantric view is an ever-widening circle of meaning, forever making new connections to new aspects of existence. The Tantric path in Buddhism is less a program of study than a series of experiments wherein the student ventures into different regions and tests the possibilities of life. To progress along the path, one must make efforts and take risks, which is one reason why Tantric masters are fond of warning Westerners against going too far without the guidance of a qualified teacher.

The vajrayana is sometimes described—in terminology reminiscent of Carlos Castaneda's works—as the "path of the warrior." It would be easy to misunderstand this, to get the impression that there is a bellicose aspect to Tibetan Buddhism. But there isn't: The warrior simile comes from the vajrayana view that every second of life is to be welcomed as the proper time for advancing in the quest, that every aspect of human behavior must be seen as holy and meaningful and rife with opportunity. This requires a warriorlike state of constant readiness, constant attention. There are times when it is necessary to confront the aspects of life that religious seekers usually avoid as too dangerous, and not to get caught by them; the follower of the path becomes a spiritual bullfighter, deliberately taking risks.

The body plays an extremely important part in the vajrayana. "Tantricism," as an Indian scholar puts it, "lays stress upon a fundamental postulate that truth resides within the body . . . in other words, the human body is the best medium through which truth is to be realized."[4] However, it is never *only* the body that is involved in vajrayana work; from the Buddhist perspective there is no such thing as an exclusively physical act. The practices are integrative, involving the body and the mind and a third element, speech. The Buddhist texts sometimes speak of the "precious human body," which is consistent with the larger Buddhist concept of the great cosmic significance of human life—that to be human is to be in a unique and precious situation, not to be wasted.

The emphasis on the body in vajrayana practice also expresses the Tibetan Buddhist notion that enlightenment—or, let us say, higher consciousness, or a fuller experience of life—cannot come from outside yourself. It is all there, in the existing body/mind, and the path is not a process of acquiring something that was not previously one's own but rather one of exploring your own being. "The vajrayana," the fourteenth-century Tibetan sage Longchenpa wrote, "emphasizes the goal which is already present now and is in our mind."[5]

Although the vajrayana has its strenuous side, it also has, if you look at it from a slightly different perspective, a yielding, accepting, almost Taoist feel to it. It says, Let things be; open up to all the parts of yourself and life; remove the blocks and allow reality to flow through your conscious awareness. Although you may be asked to work hard, to concentrate, to focus your energy on a task, you are also advised to avoid getting into conflicts with yourself. You are dealing with your own human nature, and you are not to go after it like a boxer, trying to knock it out of the ring; rather, you are to learn how to flow skillfully with its energies, like a master of the Oriental martial arts.

The idea of spiritual practice that seeks to harmonize with human nature rather than overwhelm it is common in the Orient, but it runs hard against Western consciousness. The obstacle is not merely the old Christian notion of the corruption of the flesh; that is a relatively easy concept for us to understand, smile at, and put down as something that we are now beyond. Our real problem is the deeper belief, anchored in the bedrock of even the hippest American mind, that there is something inherently wrong with everybody— that some part of the self must be stamped out. This error is the creation of the ego-centered, samsaric mind, which cannot discriminate between a human being and its self-image.

In our everyday, nonsectarian discourse such thinking is generally expressed in statements about the lower or brute aspects of human nature that have to be overcome by the higher parts of it, usually called "civilized." In Freudian psychoanalysis it is presented in terms of the struggle between id and superego, in which the superego functions, as Freud once put it, like a prudent ruling class that has to hold down the energies of a pleasure-mad and potentially destructive mob.[6] It is even present—in fact, very conspicuously—in the current wave of American spirituality, which often seems to take the form of a battle between the right-thinking new-age higher consciousness and the bad-habit-besotted lower consciousness. Whatever window you may be looking through, you are still dealing with the assumption that the essential characteristic of human life—especially of personal growth —is conflict. The Buddhists say it isn't necessarily so. There

are patterns of behavior that may not be working for you,
true, but you do not have to become your own enemy in
order to get somewhere. Human nature is on your side. Nature is on your side.

Consider the way Tibetan Buddhism approaches the
problem presented by the forms of behavior that we can't
seem to control—drug or alcohol abuse, for example, or
some recurrent pattern of sexual misconduct. The Tantric
tradition in Tibetan Buddhism offers three alternative ways
of dealing with troublesome behavior patterns: These are
characterized as vanquishing, ennobling, and yielding.[7]

"Vanquishing" is the "cold-turkey" approach to self-
improvement. In some cases the problem—smoking, for example—must be overcome by an act of will. When it is successful, it is like clearing away a growth of underbrush and
allowing new plants to grow. But it may not work, may be
worse than the "problem." The difficulty, as Western psy-
chotherapists have also discovered, is that the problem may
have very deep sources that cannot be taken care of simply
by removing the symptom. Also, the problem, viewed from
a slightly different perspective, may not be a problem at
all. The vajrayana, then, is far different from the American
"behavior-mod" eagerness to amputate any personal characteristic or behavior pattern that fails to meet society's
expectations. The vajrayana is likely to prescribe other
methods.

"Ennobling" can be simply a matter of transferring the
emotional drive directly toward a more appropriate object;
in this case it resembles what we call "sublimation," as when
frustrated sexual energies are displaced into artistic creation.
Ennobling may also utilize the more complex—and typically
Tantric—practice of deliberately creating visual images to
serve as inner targets for emotional energy. This practice is
one of the stranger and more difficult aspects of Buddhist
psychological technology, and it makes sense only within
the context of Buddhist ideas regarding desire.

Buddhism consistently stresses the mental, intentional, and participatory aspects of desire. When you want something, you are investing your own energies heavily in the experience; in a sense, you are actively creating the feeling of need within yourself and projecting desirability toward another object. Buddhism recognizes the basic biological needs (which of course you should attend to), but from the Buddhist perspective no desires are simply physical; desire, for a human being, always invokes mental activity. Hunger and sexual craving, for example, are sophisticated intellectual productions in which cultural values, self-images, and other abstract notions have much influence. There is also—as you learn from Buddhist mindfulness practice—an element of personal choice in any decision to fix your attention on an object of desire and keep it there. Buddhism does not indulge the "prisoner of desire" image that is so popular in the Western romantic tradition; it insists that you are also the prison builder, warden, guard, and gatekeeper.

Therefore, recognizing that the ego-centered and essentially insatiable samsaric mind has helped to create the whole business—desire, object and all—the Tantric adept performs one of those acts of psychological hocus-pocus that are characteristic of Tibetan Buddhism: He or she deliberately creates an imaginary mental image to take up the emotional energy that has been going into the troublesome behavior pattern; the force is withdrawn from one object and transferred to the other. The mental image that is created—with the vividness that results from years of practice in visualization—may be a beautiful female figure if the troublesome passion is sexual desire, a fierce warrior if the difficulty is anger. Tibetan art is rich with such images, and though I would certainly advise the interested Westerner to study such works of art, I would not suggest using them. They are the products of Tibetan culture, and I doubt that the Western male is likely to have much luck affixing his lust to the oddly colored ladies who float through the skies in

Tibetan tapestries, or to be able to come home from the office and release his pent-up anger at an image of a medieval Oriental warlord.

In any case, the created image is not in itself the end of the ennobling practice; it is only the staging ground for the next step. Once you have created a clear and complete visualized image and projected the emotional content into it, you are then supposed to transfer that energy again, now that you have domesticated it, to a primary life goal. The love/sex energy flows into the goal of full liberation; the hate/anger energy goes against the obstacles in the way of obtaining it. One of the basic principles of the vajrayana is that no emotion is to be repressed or blocked from awareness—but sooner or later all emotional energy must be harnessed and put to work for higher life purposes; that is what the ennobling practice is about.

"Yielding," the third strategy, leads to such practices as the ritualized sexual act that is sometimes mistaken to be the whole of tantrism. Yielding basically has to do with paying attention, being mindful.

Mindfulness practice, which has been from the beginning the center of the Buddhist way of experiencing life, deals with something many of us have discovered independently: that our adventures in hedonism—the pleasures we try so hard to obtain, the ecstatic experiences we try so hard to re-create exactly as they once were—often turn out to be rather flat, if not downright unpleasant. We notice that for the compulsive eater the act of eating is a rather joyless one; the food seems to pass directly from the plate to the stomach with scarcely a pause in the mouth, where its taste can be savored. We see the alcoholic plunging into misery in search of a replay of some long-gone moment of drunken happiness. We observe that our sexual activities are cluttered with fantasy, expectations, intellectualizations, self-images, and disappointments. All of this has to do with not being *here*, with not being aware of precisely what is happening at the moment it is happening. It also has to do with believing it is ever possible to re-create an experience, a belief that tags along behind belief in a permanent self.

So in its simplest form the Tantric Buddhist prescription is to yield: Go ahead and do it, whatever it is, if you think you must and it doesn't harm somebody else. But pay attention; be fully aware of what goes on in your mind and body, of how it really feels. And remember that everything changes. You are not the person you were a year ago, or yesterday. Relax and observe reality without preconceptions. Enjoy experience as it is, and not as you think it should be. Welcome surprises, and don't be greedy.

All of this is elementary, and easy for non-Buddhists to understand and test out in their own lives. The ritualized aspects of the Tantric yielding practice get a good deal fancier, but the principle behind them is an uncomplicated expression of the vajrayana attitude toward life, which stresses awareness and sees all things as equally sacred. Ritual, first of all, is in itself a mindfulness practice; it is a way you call your own attention to the thing you are doing. The daily life of Buddhists in Tibet—both in the monasteries and among the lay people—was punctuated by rituals. For the devout vajrayana practitioner almost every act—going to bed, waking up, eating, and even defecating—can be elaborated by ritual also.

Consider a mealtime in a Tibetan Buddhist meditation center. The serving of any meal is enhanced by simple rituals: A mantra is chanted, then the meal is taken in silence. Everyone sits down together at the same time, rises at the same time. It is nothing elaborate, yet the ritual frames the time of eating and draws the attention into the place and the business at hand. For a while you are just eating and not doing anything else. It is a rather different experience from eating a Big Mac while you are driving on the freeway and listening to the radio.

A ritual can be a mindfulness practice or it can be just

the opposite, depending on how you relate to it and to the tradition of which it is a part. We have all had the experience of participating in stagnant rituals, ceremonies that are devoid of meaning or emotional content for us. Although the Tantric Buddhist tradition is perfectly open to the idea of people's participating in some rituals without understanding what they are about, the higher vajrayana practices are clearly meant to be understood and felt at many levels.

The vajrayana path is a deliberate mobilization of the resources of body and mind for the purpose of exploring human existence. In this sense it is rather like constructing the vehicle and finding the fuel to venture into outer space. However, the vajrayana teaching strongly stresses the importance of feeling and attitude; its inner technology involves the life and growth of a human being, not the impersonal clanking of machinery. The vajrayana perpetuates the ancient Buddhist values of selflessness and compassion; it also requires an openness toward life, a sense of tolerance, a balance of confidence and humility. Traditional Buddhist morality, like that of Christianity, regards pride as a sin; but in the vajrayana a certain kind of pride, "Tantric pride," is regarded highly. This is not the pride of the personal ego but a sense of awe and respect for the enormous evolutionary force that expresses itself through human life. From this perspective a certain confidence is appropriate. "The universe," as Tarthang Tulku puts it, "is confident."

The first step along the vajrayana path, then, is to develop the proper intellectual and emotional orientation toward such an odyssey in personal exploration. The next is to acquire the necessary concentration and patience that will enable you to become proficient in the use of its nonmechanical tools.

Visualization—learning to hold certain patterns of form and color in the mind—is one of those tools. Like other aspects of Tibetan Buddhism, it is only a different way of making use of a natural human capacity. We all have some native ability to create visual images in our mind, and we know that some people have more of a knack for it than others. For some people—artists, designers, navigators—the ability to visualize is an important occupational skill. We don't ordinarily think of visualization as a gateway to new dimensions of consciousness, however; nor do we have much in the way of techniques for developing the ability. In the vajrayana, visualization training is essential: I doubt very much that a spiritual tradition that was not strongly visually oriented would have taken for itself such a striking name as the "diamond vehicle."

Training in visualization can begin with a very easy and

The Tibetan letter ah, *a symbol of shunyata.*

pleasant exercise. For example: Close your eyes and imagine a field of some lovely color, such as a rich turquoise blue. Do not fight with yourself about it if the color comes and goes, but let yourself believe it is there and experience its nourishing coolness.

As you continue the practice, you usually use as an aid a drawing of the image or symbol to be visualized. (Later you will dispense with such devices.) Students at the Nyingma Institute are given small white-on-black graphic representations, about three inches high, of the Tibetan letter *ah*, which represents shunyata. The instruction is: About six times a day, for periods of twenty minutes each, concentrate on the symbol by tracing its outline from left to right. After two days of this, begin concentrating on the whole image. This is to be done for a total of fifty hours or so, by which time you should be able to picture it with your eyes closed. You will later learn to reduce the image in size and picture it resting in a specific part of your body.

Although some people simply do not take to visualization at all, most find that it has definite pleasant results that begin to pay off well this side of Buddhahood. It produces clearly discernible states of freshness and relaxation, and, perhaps of greater interest to most of us, the concentration skills acquired through visualization practice are transferable to other realms of activity such as studying, or playing golf. Most forms of worldly success require the ability to concentrate; the superworldly goal of Buddhism is pursued largely through learning to concentrate. And from the vajrayana point of view you are perfectly welcome to pursue worldly success while you are on the way to becoming enlightened.

The shunyata meditation is an elementary example of visualization training. The advanced vajrayana practioner must learn to visualize extremely complex images, such as the deities that appear in Tibetan works of art and the intricate meditation devices called *mandalas.* Such images are to be held in the consciousness clearly, with all details in place.

The student must also develop a heightened awareness of certain centers in the body, the *chakras.* These are part of all esoteric religions, although different schools may emphasize different centers. Among the Sufis, for example, the emphasis is on the navel, the heart, and the head; hence the Islamic gesture of touching the hand to the head, heart, and stomach and then extending it outward. Yoga teaches of seven main centers reaching from the base of the spine to the top of the head, as well as several secondary centers. Zen, with characteristic simplicity, uses one: Zen meditators learn to focus on the spot called the *hara*, in the stomach, just below the navel. Vajrayana practice concentrates on four centers: the navel, the heart, the throat, and the head. Each is held to be the locus of certain properties: Compassion is usually identified with the heart; thought, with the head, and so on.

None of this is entirely alien to Western consciousness. We believe that thinking goes on in the brain, and neurological research is quite precise in locating certain functions in certain parts of the brain. Science is not yet ready to locate emotions in the heart, but all our popular songs and St. Valentine's Day cards suggest that we have an intuitive awareness of the connection. There are hints of a similar intuitive sense of the significance of the navel in our talk of gut feelings and visceral awareness. We don't seem to have any comparable folk wisdom about the throat center, although *Deep Throat* may change that; any student of esoteric religion would get a chuckle out of the idea of a zone of intense erotic stimulation located in the spot known to vajrayana lore as the *sambhoga-chakra*, the "center of bliss."

With the multidimensionality that is typical of Tantric practice, meditation upon the chakras may invoke sounds, colors, and meanings. In one meditation the head chakra is to be visualized in connection with the syllable *om*, the color white, and all the dharmas categorized as belonging to the *rupa-skandha*—those involving form. The throat chakra has the syllable *ah*, the color red, and the samjna-skandha of consciousness or sensation. The heart chakra has the syllable *hum*, a deep-blue color and the vijnana-skandha of perceptions. The navel is identified with the syllable *sva*, yellow, and the vedana-skandha of feelings. Since there are five skandhas in the Abhidharma, a fifth center is required, and in this particular meditation the consciousness is to be centered in both feet, simultaneously with the syllable *ha*, the color green, and the samskara-skandha involving impulses. The advanced meditator learns to hold all these centers in the consciousness at once, together with the appropriate sounds, colors, and meanings. This can be made yet more complex with the addition of other elements, such as deities, that correspond to each chakra.

The physical aspect of Tantric meditation practice also uses body positions and gestures known as *mudras*. Many of the hand mudras are shown in Buddhist art; in some paintings of the Buddha he is shown with his left hand resting on his lap in the gesture of meditation, the *dhyana-mudra*, while his right hand touches the earth in the *bhumisparisa-mudra*.

The mudras are symbols, but to call them merely symbolic is to miss the point of their real significance in vajrayana practice. A mudra is understood to be functionally related to a certain state of consciousness; the cause-and-effect sequence is not clear, so it would not be exactly right to say that it either expresses a state or creates it; it is a sign that that state exists. Tantric lore contains a great lexicon of mudras, and they all have specific meanings and cross references to sounds and colors with which they are identified. Some vajrayana rituals employ highly complex sequences of hand gestures.[8]

Mudras are known to the West and to Western religion; the familiar gesture of putting the hands together in prayer is a mudra; so is the Catholic sign of the cross, which also closely resembles the Islamic three-chakra salutation. The familiar "peace sign" used by friendly Indians in the movies happens to be precisely the same as the mudra known in Tantric Buddhism as the "gesture of fearlessness."

Some vajrayana meditations combine gestures with mantras, either spoken aloud or intoned silently in conjunction with the breath. For example, one meditation uses the syllables *om*, *ah*, and *hum*. You sit cross-legged with the hands resting palms up on the knees and silently imagine *om* as the breath is taken in and the hands are turned palms down. Pausing after the inhalation (that space between breaths is held to be an especially good opportunity to glimpse the truth of shunyata) you bring the fingertips to the center of the chest with the syllable *ah* heard in the mind. Exhaling with the syllable *hum* in mind, you extend the hands outward in a gesture of giving and then rest the hands palms up on the knees. Turn the hands over with the next inhalation, and proceed with the meditation for twenty minutes or so. This meditation may be made more complex, with the addition of visualization elements; or, as a simple calming procedure, it can be done anywhere for a few minutes without the gestures.

Mantras, such as the *om ah hum*, are another basic tool in Tantric practice. Perhaps the most famous mantra associated with Tibetan Buddhism is *om mani padme hum*, which is usually translated as "Hail to the jewel in the lotus." This isn't quite accurate, since *om* signifies the infinite cosmos and the principle of enlightenment, but the central words *mani* (jewel) and *padme* (lotus) do convey the essence of the mantra. They can be interpreted several ways; for example, the jewel can represent enlightenment and the lotus the human mind. Mantras do not lend themselves to easy translation. Anagarika Govinda, a European who became a Tibetan Buddhist lama, has written a 300-page book that is mainly an exposition of the meaning of *om mani padme hum*.[9] Another mantra (particularly important at the Nyingma school, since it is identified with Guru Padmasambhava, the eighth-century teacher who is regarded as the special patron of that lineage) is *om ah hum vajra guru padma siddhi hum*. *Vajra* means "diamond" (and also shunyata); guru means "wisdom" or "teacher"; padma is "lotus"; and siddhi is "power." The *hum* syllable is a complement to *om* in several mantras. *Om* signifies a reaching outward; *hum*, a reaching inward to the heart center.

Most mantras have literal meanings, but the meanings are never the total content; the sound is at least as important. The syllables are believed to have precise vibrational qualities that can, in the proper circumstances, produce certain states of consciousness. The meanings relate to these states.

In vajrayana practice all the pieces—the sounds, the gestures, the visualizations—flow together and create kaleidoscopic patterns of feeling and meaning. John Blofeld speaks of this:

> Tantric symbols invariably interpenetrate; again and again one comes across symbols which hint at the meanings of other symbols and yet others, thereby symbolizing the interpenetration of every aspect of the universe. The effect of Tantric studies is like that of breaking open a ball in which is discovered a second and in that a third and so on until one comes to what seems to be a solid centre; but it breaks at a touch and inside it is found precisely that ball which had originally enclosed them all; then the whole sequence is repeated again and again until Enlightenment dawns. One gets an impression of meanings within meaning and, above all, of the presence of the whole in each of its parts.[10]

All this expresses the Tantric view of a universe that is intricately interconnected, and also alive, vibrating with sound and color and meaning. The complexity can be overwhelming at first, which is one reason why beginning students of vajrayana are usually well advised to start with a simple meditation practice before leaping into any of the texts on Tantric symbolism. In time the parts begin to come together; you begin to see the figure in the carpet, and then any of the Tantric devices can become, like the famous tea cake in Proust's *Remembrance of Things Past,* the key to a rich world of inner experience.

Remember that the vajrayana is Tibetan Buddhism and that its purpose is not merely to polish up the sensibilities of an ego-centered self; it is meant to transform and transcend ordinary concepts of who and what you are. It is not to enable you to see the universe in a more interesting fashion but to enable you to understand that you are a prism through which the universe sees itself.

The diamond symbol suggests the many-faceted and sparkling quality of reality; but vajra also stands for shunyata, for clear space, the void, emptiness, "no-thing-ness." In the Tibetan Buddhist cosmology this pristine nothingness is the source of all the interesting and richly meaningful reality that we find about us, which we can, if we choose, learn to experience in ever more vivid and profound subtlety. As we do so, we sense more accurately that beneath this reality is something—or nothing—indescribable, from which it emerges. The vajrayana symbol, used in many rites and usually present on the meditation altar in Tibetan homes, is the diamond scepter, which is actually two diamond-shaped extremities connected at the center by a sphere. The sphere represents the undifferentiated source of being, and the two poles are the basic energies that issue from it. Coming out of the sphere are two lotuses, with prongs extending from them: polarized energies vibrating out of a common ground of being. For the Tibetan Buddhist the entire cosmos is a vast magic show reflected from emptiness. It is not unreal; nor is it always what it might appear to be. It is not created by your mind, yet your mind can participate in the shaping of it.

The psychophysical technology of Tantric practice is ultimately meant to enable you to see through the illusory

The vajra, *or "diamond scepter," representing the polarized*
energies of consciousness that radiate from
an undifferentiated center.

nature of being to its reality; along the way, your consciousness may learn to play some audacious games with its own
content. For example, let us take a look at two advanced
forms of Tantric practice: the invocation of deities, and the
conscious transformation of ordinary experience.

   The vajrayana method of visualizing quasihuman
beings for redirecting emotional energies (the ennobling
practice) is only a limited and specialized form of a larger
body of practices that, taken altogether, form a fascinating
psychology that is still little known in the West.

Before we proceed further into this subject, let us briefly browse through some of our own ideas regarding imaginary beings. We are familiar with the history of religious visions in the Christian tradition, with the imaginary playmates of children, with the various beings that invade the consciousness of mentally ill people, and with the figures that come to us in dreams. We know that such "imagined" entities can take on great importance, at times become even more significant forces in our lives than real people. We also have, of course, all the old gods and goddesses of mythological lore, beings that were once, in other times and places, quite "real" but that we now commonly take to be nothing more than manifestations of the unconscious mind. Then, of course, we have the venerable folklore of magic, recently returned to life in a flood of books and movies about demons and devils and exorcists. All this adds up to a sizable amount of descriptive information about such phenomena, although we generally don't accord it much credibility. In the vajrayana, however, the native human ability to imagine and visualize such beings is valued, developed, and made a central part of life.

Tibetan Buddhist literature often refers to female spirits who appear either spontaneously or as a result of deliberate meditative effort. There seems to be a certain historical progression involved here: In the earlier writings, such as the biographies of the "great sorcerers" of vajrayana lore, the female images usually appear of their own volition and in horrendous, wrathful forms, even though they often provide help and information. Later Tibetan writings give instructions on how to summon up visions of female spirits, and they are more frequently depicted as peaceful, benevolent, and beautiful. Tibetan Buddhism gradually developed a whole body of meditative and ritualistic practice built around female spirits. The most important of these, the green goddess Tara, is the object of many rituals and occupies a position in Tibetan Buddhism somewhat analogous to that of the Virgin Mary in Christianity. The distinctive aspect of Tibetan Buddhism is not the presence of a female spirit as an object of devotion—which is common to many religions—but the meditation practice in which the individual student contacts his own personal female spirit: She may be the Tara or any of the multitude of spirits inherited by the vajrayana from Indian tantrism and the old Tibetan Bön, and she may be either wrathful or benevolent according to the psychological needs of the students, as determined by the guru. The student learns to visualize this personal spirit, known as a *yidam*,* invokes her image in daily meditations, and relies on her as a source of inspiration and guidance. I am told that in such practices the student is given to understand that the yidam is a product of the imagination, but that she is nonetheless to be regarded both emotionally and intellectually. She fulfills some of the functions of the idealized sex-fantasy images so familiar to the Western male, and also seems to have much in common with our ideas of the muse or guardian angel, except that the yidam is no object of relaxed reverie. The student expends much effort on learning how to invoke the image vividly and is taught to respect her as a significant figure in his life.

Since this aspect of Tibetan Buddhism was discovered by the West many writers have noted its apparent similarity to one of the main themes of Jungian psychology: the "anima," the "female within the male," the archetypal force within the unconscious mind that can manifest itself in many forms—as dream symbol, as the genesis of psychopathology, or as a force of inspiration.[11] And Jungian therapy, like vajrayana practice, counsels making contact with the female part of the personality:

The art of it consists only in allowing our invisible partner to make herself heard, in putting the mechanism of expression

* *Yidam* is the term for the personal deity. The general class of female deities is called *daikini* in Sanskrit, *khadomas* in Tibetan.

momentarily at her disposal, without being overcome by the distaste one naturally feels at playing such an apparently ludicrous game with oneself. . . .[12]

This "apparently ludicrous game," as Jung put it, is a serious lifelong pursuit of the student of Tantric Buddhism; the yidam for the advanced meditator becomes a personage no less important than his "real" teachers.

I have been deliberately employing the masculine gender in this discussion because the visualization of female images by male practitioners is definitely the predominant part of the literature on the subject. But the vajrayana also recognizes male spirits, just as Jungian theory recognizes the "animus," the male segment of the female psyche. And visualization practice does not always involve figures of the opposite sex: Female students might learn to invoke female figures, and male students might work with male images, depending on their individual needs.

The Jungian and vajrayana traditions both urge some caution and prudence in dealing with these images. In Jungian therapy the anima can be a source of neurosis, even madness, if not properly integrated into the consciousness. Tibetan Buddhist writings repeatedly warn against going too far with any such practices except under the supervision of a qualified teacher. It is not hard to understand why: The act of dealing with imaginary beings as if they were real is precisely the same as what we would call "hallucinatory psychosis." The difference is largely in the state of mind that precipitates the experience. "The yogin," as one Western student of Tibetan Buddhism notes, "goes forth to add a reality to his repertoire of awareness; he does not create one universe in frightened retreat from another." His power to summon up powerful and lifelike beings, then, is based upon "his understanding and hence upon his control of himself and his reality; the schizophrenic's power is based not on control but on chaos."[13]

The chief obstacle to Western understanding of such practices is not likely to be in accepting (at least provisionally) the reports that Tibetan Buddhist contemplatives do develop the ability to visualize such beings in detail and that the beings play an important part in their lives. None of this goes too far beyond territory that most of us are familiar with. The tricky part is the question of whether the apparitions are real or not.

The subject is not likely to make Westerners uncomfortable as long as it is stipulated that we are talking about something that is psychological, meaning that it has no particular claim to being *real*. As Jung once noted, "Whenever a Westerner hears the word 'psychological,' it always sounds to him like *only* psychological."[14] By identifying something as the product of the imagination or the subconscious, we conclude that it does not "really" exist in the external world.

Or, if you have a more occult turn of mind, you might prefer to think that all the demons and goddesses really do inhabit the world, unseen by most of us, and reveal themselves—sometimes of their own volition, sometimes when properly summoned—to certain people.

I fear that neither of these accurately represents Tibetan Buddhism. In the vajrayana world view the mind is a participant in the creation of all phenomena, inner and outer, and even the hard, public, "objective" occupants of the cosmos are in a sense unreal and dreamlike images. All reality is relative, an interaction of the mind with something that cannot be defined except in terms of our experience of it. The Tibetan contemplative, conjuring up his yidam, is participating in an act of the imagination and also contacting a reality.

These same powers of imagination are used consciously to alter the nature of everyday experience. The basic elements of this practice are contained in the dharma psychology, and the first steps can be taken experientially in meditation: You may discover that from time to time you enter states of consciousness that because of their unfamiliarity seem unpleasant. Vajrayana meditation practice teaches subtle exercises, rather like placing the weight on one foot and then the other, in which you learn to experience the state first as unpleasant and then as pleasant. You can try a similar mood-switching experiment in some ordinary moment of the day: In any situation imagine how it would feel if you were in an especially high physical and emotional state, as if you had just heard a great piece of news; then try putting an equally unpleasant construction on the same situation, and see what happens as you deliberately switch back and forth between the two.

Tibetan Buddhist teaching does not advise you to leap from this practice into the Pollyanna-ish assumption that a simple act of imagination can keep you permanently happy. You are simply testing the proposition, central to Buddhist psychology, that the feeling-tones of a situation are largely determined by the intellectual construction that you put on it. The exercise gives you an opportunity to *see* this process at work, and also provides an opportunity to flex your mental muscles in preparation for other experiments.

In Tibetan Buddhist practice the adept learns to transform everyday reality through a deliberate act of consciousness: Every being is to be seen as a mysterious deity; every voice is to be heard as the teaching of a guru; every sound, a mantra; every moment, an opportunity for profound learning; every part of the surroundings, the perfect reflections of the diamondlike essence of reality. This is a trick, of course, but from the Buddhist perspective it is a trick played upon another trick; it is meant to divert attention from the samsaric mind that locks us into unsatisfactory experiences and blocks us from seeing the cosmos truly full of magic and meaning, precisely as the adept imagines it to be.

5. The Body on the Spiritual Path: Relaxation, Health, and Healing

Tibetan Buddhist ideas about the body resemble, in some ways, the psychotherapy of Wilhelm Reich. Reich's work in character analysis led him to the view that character itself is a disorder, a hardening of the fluid human reality into a fixed and limiting pattern of behavior. He believed this was a physical problem as well as a mental one: The body, expressing the mind's rigidity, developed "character armor" as a defense against the fearful uncertainties of life and, inevitably, against its own feelings. Reich became convinced that since emotional problems had physical manifestations, they could be attacked through the use of physical techniques. He began to use breathing exercises and massage in psychotherapy.

In the Tibetan Buddhist view the ego is a limitation of human reality, and a physical problem as well as a mental and spiritual one. Holding on to a rigid self-image, struggling to censor and manipulate your experience to meet its demands, is hard work. There is physical tension, and physical pain. The basic discomfort that the Buddha referred to in the first noble truth can be easily understood as a physical condition—the more or less persistent bodily tension that is so familiar a part of life for nearly all of us. And how better to understand samsara, the "going around in circles" of ego-centered life, than to look at the way a team of American doctors described the heart-attack-prone "type A" personality:

> He will always feel the need to be accomplishing something, and to be engaged in some activity he considers constructive, so as not to waste a single minute of precious time. Time literally becomes the Type A individual's enemy, since he is always trying to beat it by setting unrealistic deadlines. He may create undue time pressure for himself in tasks ranging from getting out a report, cleaning out the attic, beating the commuter traffic home at night, to swimming his daily exercise laps in the pool. His competition with the clock is unrelieved. . . .[1]

The term the doctors use for the behavior of the "type A" person—"hurry sickness"—is a more eloquent translation of samsara than any Buddhist scholar has yet come up with.

So the conditions that Tibetan Buddhism addresses itself to are not just disembodied philosophical notions but also physical problems. This is something we can understand: Western medicine is developing a much clearer picture of the damage that is done to the body by anxiety and stress; we are finding out that in many ways people are literally destroying themselves. We are beginning to understand that people are so driven by socially conditioned self-expectations, so fenced in by deluded notions of what they are, that they set up emotional forces that contribute to heart disease, ulcers, cancer, diabetes, and a host of other ailments. This knowledge puts us in a much better position to understand Buddhism. It turns out that the ego sickness hurts; samsara kills.

Thus the path to enlightenment involves dealing with physical states as well as mental ones. It is not only a matter of becoming wise but also a matter of becoming relaxed. Relaxation and physical health are considered to be preconditions to enlightenment; or, to put it another way, enlightenment is considered to be a relaxed and healthy state. It is a condition of full aliveness, the way you are meant to be. The vajrayana concept of the body as a source of deep, genetically encoded wisdom, as a vehicle for self-exploration, also carries the condition that the body is a most precious instrument that needs to be well cared for.

Tibetan Buddhism, especially for the beginner, emphasizes the importance of simply taking care of yourself. You are not made to feel guilty about your sins; nor are you urged to embark forthwith upon some strenuous program of spiritual adventure. Instead, you are invited to ease up a little, give yourself some quiet time, pay attention to what you are doing to yourself, see how your body is feeling. The higher states of consciousness described by Tibetan Buddhists do not sound like psychedelic frenzies but like conditions of peace and openness and clarity. Longchenpa, one of the great sages of the vajrayana, continually speaks of enlightenment as the mind's comfort and ease.

THE NYINGMA INSTITUTE teaches a system of relaxation practices called *kum nye*, which admirably express this philosophy. They can be used as aids to self-healing, or as a warm-up for a period of meditation.

Since for many people the attempt to meditate is seriously hindered by physical tensions, working with the body first is an effective way to go more deeply into concentration when sitting. But the kum-nye exercises do not necessarily have to be used for this purpose, or done in a complete sequence. You can do them for a half hour before meditation, or for five minutes before a business meeting.

I will describe here a simple series of kum-nye exercises that can easily be performed by the beginner as a way of finding out how they work.* I suggest that they be done slowly, allowing as much as a half hour for the series of movements, followed by a half hour of sitting meditation. This produces a state of deep calm that normally lasts for about a day; if the practice is done regularly, that state will be experienced a good part of the time. I don't mean to suggest that an hour a day of kum nye and meditation is the end to tension forever, but the practices do produce results. That is what the concept of karma is about: All your actions really do have consequences.

State of mind is an important factor in the effectiveness of kum-nye practices. Although some of them require vigorous movement, they should not be done as a mighty act of willpower, as competition with yourself or others. They do not even have to be thought of as a personal skill that you have achieved. They are simply something you learn how to do, like brushing your teeth. You do them conscientiously, but they are nothing special. You do them with a sense of taking care of yourself. Even a little compassion for your own tense body might be in order. I have yet to find anything in the Buddhist writings about compassion that forbids you to feel it toward yourself. With that in mind, let us try some Tibetan exercises.

1. Stretching. Stand in a comfortable position and extend your arms straight upward from the shoulders in a pushing motion, as if you were lifting a weight. Allow the fingers to be relaxed, and push mainly with the palms and heels of the hands. Stretch up as far as you can; then bring the hands

* These and other kum-nye exercises are illustrated in the Appendix, p. 199.

down to shoulder level, but keep the palms up. Repeat this at least five times, making the movement progressively more vigorous. Imagine each time that you are lifting a heavier weight. Then let the arms hang down loosely for a minute. While you do, pay attention to them and see how they are feeling.

Now, using the same hand shape—fingers relaxed, palm and heels doing the pushing—stretch straight forward, as if pushing something away. Repeat this movement several times, and experiment with different levels of intensity— from very elegant, gentle, subtle stretches without effort to vigorous ones involving chest and shoulder muscles. Relax, and again direct attention to the muscles you have been working with to see how they feel.

In the final segment of this exercise, keeping the arms at about chest level, push first to one side and then to the other, turning the waist so that both hands are on about the same plane. Again experiment with degrees of intensity; as you develop your awareness of this dimension of the exercises you will be able to vary them according to what your body needs at any given time. Sometimes you may prefer a soft, calming motion, and other times you might want a more energetic, tension-discharging level. Relax at the end of the sequence, and allow your attention to stay for a minute with the feeling you have produced.

2. *Hang and back bend.* Stand with the feet about the same distance apart as the width of your shoulders, and bend forward from the waist so that your arms and head hang down. Breathe deeply and gently in this position, allowing the arms and head to swing loosely and become heavy. Hold the position for a few minutes, allowing your body to relax into it.

Then bend backward, putting your hands against the buttocks or small of the back, to give yourself some support.

Bend the knees slightly, and drop the head back so you are looking behind you. In this position, very gently move the upper part of the body up and down in a sort of bouncing motion, letting yourself bend backward a bit farther with the movement if it feels comfortable.

Bend over forward again, and repeat the sequence until you have done it at least three times. Then just stand for a minute with your eyes closed and breathe easily.

3. Punch and jump. This is the most strenuous exercise of the series, and should be done energetically. Stand as before, and then, with a quick jump, step forward with the left foot and backward with the right. At the same time, straighten out your right arm, fist clenched, in front of you and draw back the left arm so it is cocked at the side, ready to punch. You should now be in an exaggerated boxer's position, looking somewhat like an old photograph of John L. Sullivan, and your left foot should be far enough forward so that you feel a good stretch in the legs.

With one quick jump, reverse the position. Now your right foot is forward and the left foot back. The left arm is extended in a straight punch, and the right arm pulled back alongside the waist. Repeat this until you have done both motions at least five times. If it feels good, do it fifteen or twenty times, and try turning as you jump so that you come down at about a 45-degree angle to your previous position. You can go in a full circle with this, and perhaps discover that the exercise feels best to you when you are pointed in a certain direction.

After you have finished, stand for a moment before you proceed to the next part.

4. Self-massage: hands and forearms. There are a number of self-massage sequences in kum nye. This one is designed to reach some of the major acupuncture "command points" and also to take care of a part of the body that frequently builds up muscle tension without your being aware of it.

Get yourself into a comfortable seated position, either cross-legged on the floor or in a chair. Allow the left hand to lie loosely on your lap, palm upward, and begin to massage it with the right. As you would if you were giving a massage to a friend, be slow, gentle, and thorough. Start with the fingers, and do each finger at a time. Then begin to work on the palm; at this point you can begin to experiment, as you would in any form of massage, with different tools; use the fingers, knuckles, or palm of your right hand. Find out if deep, powerful touching seems right for you, and also try very light, skin-stroking touches. Do the back of the hand, applying enough pressure in the web spaces to force apart gently the bones leading to the fingers. Then move upward to the wrist and forearm. If you do this part thoroughly, you will massage all the main acupuncture points. Try locating a muscle and following it upward along the arm, touching its entire surface. See if you can identify and gently massage the lateral spaces between muscles. Be sure that you do not miss any part of the forearm. With your fingertips, gently knead the sensitive nerve areas in the elbow. While you are working in this area, see if you notice any sensation in other parts of the body. Do the right hand and forearm; then work on the upper arms, and move gradually into the next sequence.

5. *Self-massage: neck and shoulders.* Using the right hand, forcefully massage the left bicep, and then move along the top of your shoulder to the base of the neck. Go back to the bicep again, and this time work along the back of the shoulder as far as the spine. Use your left hand to do the same with your right shoulder; then use both hands to massage the back of the neck. Start as far down the spine as your hands will reach, and with firm pressure move the hands away from the spine. Repeat this several times, coming a bit higher up the

neck each time. Using just the fingertips, spend some time working in the area right at the base of your skull.

6. Back rub, with a little help from your inanimate friends. You cannot easily massage your own back with your hands, but that does not mean that this important part of the body must be overlooked when you are doing self-massage. You simply make use of your environment. Try putting a pillow on the floor, beneath your back at about shoulder-blade level, which will raise your back slightly, so that your arms and legs hang down loosely and touch the floor. Lie still for a while and relax into this position until you get used to it; then move around on the pillow and use it to give yourself a back massage. When you have got the feel for this form of self-massage, you can begin to experiment with other items: Try rubbing your back against the back of a chair or the wall, or massaging your forearms against the arms of a chair. Cats, who are natural kum-nye masters, do this instinctively. Besides being a useful relaxation technique and an interesting way of relating to your environment (the world is your masseur), this practice tends to generate the proper attitude for making effective use of self-healing techniques.

7. Deep breathing and leg raises. Lie on the floor on a foam pad or soft carpet (most beds are too soft for this exercise). Your arms should be out to your sides at about a 45-degree angle, palms down. Knees are bent, legs drawn up, so that the bottoms of your feet are flat on the floor. Adjust your position and be sure you are comfortable before you begin. Pay attention to your breathing, and let it become deep and slow. Then begin the leg movements, one leg at a time, in conjunction with the breathing. The leg movements are as follows:

As you exhale, raise the left heel, keeping the ball of the foot and the toes in contact with the floor; then raise the entire foot and draw your left knee up toward the chest. The knee remains bent, so there is no tension in your lower leg or foot. As you inhale, let the left foot return to the floor; first the toes touch; then lower the heel to the floor. Then, as you exhale, raise the right leg in the same way and lower it as you inhale.

It may take you a while to get this sequence together, but you will find it easy and deeply relaxing. Be sure that you raise the leg as you exhale, lower it as you inhale. This exercise is designed to balance the life-force flow in the body.

Repeat the exercise ten times with each leg; then remain lying down for a minute before you sit up to begin the sitting meditation.

8. *Sitting meditation.* If you are already an experienced meditator, you need no special instructions for this part. Just sit in your usual way for a half hour. I do suggest, however, that you think of the sitting as being a part of the whole series. It is not a bunch of exercises followed by a period of meditation but rather a meditation which includes both moving and sitting still.

If you have not meditated before, simply get yourself into a comfortable seated position, either cross-legged on the floor or on a pillow, or seated upright in a chair. Try to find a position in which you are comfortable and your spine is erect. Either close your eyes or lower your eyelids so they are barely open, and begin to pay attention to your breath. A good beginning meditation device is to count each exhalation. Count up to ten; then start over again. When your mind begins to wander (which it will), gently bring it back to the breathing and counting.

Meditation is samadhi—mindfulness—one of the main elements of the Buddha's eightfold path. Simple sitting meditation is the basic training for all the more elaborate visualizations and mantric practices of the vajrayana path, and it is also, as Western scientists are now discovering, a health-maintaining and curative process in itself. Numerous studies have documented the effects of meditation on the physical metabolism and its ability to reduce the incidence of stress-related and psychosomatic disorders.[2]

TIBETAN APPROACHES to healing and self-healing, like the kum-nye exercises, reflect the belief that optimum well-being is a relaxed, balanced, open state. They flow from the fundamental Buddhist conviction that there is no such thing as a permanent, isolated self, and from the Tantric belief in the interconnectedness of all things. A human illness, even a minor one, is seen as a cosmic event. Yesehe Dhonden, a prominent practitioner of Tibetan medicine (and the Dalai Lama's personal physician), writes:

> As a body, man is a microcosmic but faithful reflection of the macrocosmic reality in which he is imbedded and which preserves and nourishes him every second of his life; as a mind, he is a ripple on the surface of the great ocean of consciousness.
>
> Health is the proper relationship between the microcosm which is man and the macrocosm which is the Universe. Disease is a disruption of this relationship.[3]

Although Tibet developed a complex system of medicine with elaborate diagnostic techniques, a long period of training for doctors, and a sophisticated system of pharmacology, it never looked much like its Western counterpart. Surgery was developed to a fairly high level and was practiced for several centuries, but then was abandoned. There are different explanations for why this came about. According to the popular folklore, surgery was outlawed by a king after an unsuccessful operation on the queen mother. According to the Tibetan doctor quoted above, it was found that surgery is likely to cause permanent vein and nerve damage that make it impossible for the patient to perform the more advanced vajrayana meditations involving subtle levels of awareness and control of physical processes.

There are three levels of medical practice in the Tibetan system: the "gentle methods" include simple practices such as burning incense, giving medicines or applying salves to the skin; the "stronger methods" include bloodletting and lancing abscesses; and the "violent methods" include removal of foreign bodies and cauterization of abscesses. Since internal surgery was abandoned, the list of techniques in the third category has shortened considerably. Whenever possible the Tibetan doctors prefer to use the gentler methods.

Diagnosis and care in traditional Tibetan medicine operate on several levels: They consider emotional, physical, spiritual, and ecological aspects of the disorder. A Tibetan doctor always inquires into the life situation of the patient, and may determine that the disease is an expression of some disturbance in the psychosocial environment—a death in the family, a personal misfortune, a sudden change in routine. (In this respect it resembles the comparatively recent discovery by Western researchers of the high correlation between certain stress events—such as losing a job, getting a divorce, taking out a mortgage on a house—and physical illness.[4])

When emotional conditions are deemed to be the main cause of the trouble, the prescribed remedy might be more in the way of emotional nourishment than anything else. "Catarrh, pain in the eyes, head, and heart, head spins and loss of appetite result from suppressed tears," says one Tibetan medical text. "In this case sleep, liquor and cheerful words are helpful."[5]

In most cases an extensive physiological diagnosis is carried out: The doctor examines the patient's body, analyzes urine and feces, notes sleeping and eating habits. The most important diagnostic technique in Tibetan medical practice is pulse-taking. Ideally this is done early in the morning, before dawn, and the doctor takes the pulse in each wrist. With this method a properly trained Tibetan doctor is supposed to be able to determine the condition of the heart, intestines, spleen, stomach, kidneys, lungs, liver, bladder, and reproductive organs.

When medicines are called for, the Tibetan doctor normally uses herbs, and other native materials. Herbal medicines are prepared from roots, leaves, stems, flowers, fruits, and honey; also, minerals commonly found in Tibet are used in different combinations with the herbs. In training for a medical career, a Tibetan doctor might spend years traveling through the country, learning where these materials can be found, gathering supplies of them, and becoming familiar with their uses. In practice the materials are used in different ways—boiled to produce a vapor for the patient to inhale, made into teas, or compounded into poultices. None of these remedies is expected to give a quick cure, but each is believed to have great healing powers over time, and also to be useful in many cases for preventing diseases.

Although diseases are often diagnosed as having physical causes, and treated with medicines, and descriptions of the body and the major diseases more or less resemble those known to Western medicine, Tibetan medicine does not inhabit quite the same world as our own: The leading Tibetan doctors are lamas, and their ideas of the body and the cosmos are influenced by the Tantric and yogic heritage of their religion. Their physiology deals with the organs we are familiar with, but often mentions their spiritual and emotional functions; the body also contains the chakras and the connecting channels that figure in vajrayana practices. Diseases are classified as disturbances of air, bile, and phlegm—elements that are common to the human body and to the "inanimate" natural world, and which have different effects on the system at different times of the year. In some cases an astrological reading is required to give information on the long-range karmic factors influencing the illness.

All this adds up to some rather fancy medical lore, and though many lama-doctors are extremely eminent people, the patient in Tibetan medicine never has the role of a mere passive recipient of somebody's wisdom. The patient does not simply hand his or her body over to the experts to get it repaired, but is given to understand that he or she is an active participant in the sickness and will also have to be an active participant in the cure.

The feeling-tone of the healing experience is extremely important, perhaps more important than the specific details of medical practice. A certain caring and trust has to be present, and mutually experienced. Since Tibetan medicine is inseparable from Buddhist philosophy, the supreme virtue of compassion is heavily stressed in the training of medical practitioners. The state of mind of the patient is equally important: An optimum emotional state for self-healing would include such qualities as self-compassion (which is not quite the same as self-indulgence, but a simple caring respect for your own humanness), awareness and mindfulness, a realistic understanding of the role of karma in illness (there are always a multitude of causes), and a certain cheerfulness and optimism—not blind faith that you will get well (which might not be true) but a basic confidence in the naturalness of the healing process. Dr. Dhonden, expanding on the concept that illness is a disruption of the relationship between the microcosm (the person) and the macrocosm (the universe), says simply, "Unimpeded reaction of the microcosm to such a disruption results in a cure, unless the disruption is irreversible, when death is the cure."[6]

THERE IS NOT MUCH POINT in trying to judge whether Tibetan medicine, as practiced in Tibet before 1959 and still carried on among the exiles, is better or worse than American medicine. It is "holistic," in the truest meaning of that rather overworked word: It is—or was—an integral part of Tibetan culture and Tibetan Buddhist beliefs; it treated the ailments common to the Tibetan people (apparently skin diseases were common; cancer was rare), and it used the herbs and minerals native to Tibet. Disease and its cure were at once physical, psychological, social, ecological, and spiritual events. If we understand this we can study Tibetan medicine without expecting that it can all be transplanted to the United States; some parts will take root, but some won't.

The sort of practice we might call "psychic healing" or "faith healing" definitely had an important place in Tibetan medicine. There are many accounts of lamas who were said to have miraculous healing powers, even the ability to cure diseases without being in the presence of the patient. There are similar accounts of vajrayana masters whose meditative powers and awareness of their own physiology were so advanced that they could cure themselves of the most serious ailments. (The usual devices of vajrayana practice—rituals, visualizations, mantras—are the basic technology employed in these cases.) However, writings on this subject warn that faith healings, unless performed by the most highly qualified people, produce only temporary relief if the conditions that caused the disease are not also changed. The causes—emotional, physical, spiritual, whatever—will reassert themselves, and the patient will become ill again. (Some Tibetan doctors, by the way, issue the same warning about scientific miracle cures; they warn that if, for example, we develop a cure for cancer without fully understanding it, the causes might surface in some other—and perhaps worse—form.[7])

With these reservations in mind, we can explore some of the Tibetan methods of healing. They are to be approached as explorations in meditation, applied gently without getting our egos involved in exaggerated ideas of our power to heal. And we should remember that an illness may simply have to run its course, or be cured by changing the circumstances that caused it.

Let us say, then, that you have completed some basic

practice in meditation, and would like to try to relieve pain
in somebody you care about who is suffering from localized
muscle pains caused by tension or too much exercise. Have
the person lie or sit down comfortably, so you can easily
touch the affected area; sit next to him or her for a while,
quietly. Sit with your eyes open, and notice the sounds in
the place where you are. Try listening with your eyes—this
is said to create the proper change of consciousness that in-
creases your healing abilities. Another healing meditation,
which requires considerably more practice, is to visualize a
globe of green light, about the size of a pea, in the "third-eye
point," just between the two eyes; the light should be a clear
green, darker in color toward its center. Meditate on that
light, think of it as a healing energy that you have created,
and let your consciousness at the same time become aware
of the person next to you and the pain he or she is feeling.
Remember that compassion is the key to the Buddhist philosophy of healing; you have to care about the other person's pain, so much that you would be willing to take it on
yourself.

Begin rubbing the hands together briskly, just in front
of your heart center. They will become warm, and you may
notice that if you move the palms a few inches apart, you
will feel an energy flow between them, like a magnetic attraction. Experiment with this for a while and then gently
place your hands on the part of the body where the pain is
located, keeping them there as long as it feels right to you.

Note that the situation you have brought into existence
here is one of contact, caring, and relaxation; it is—whatever
your personal threshold of doubt or belief regarding chakras
and green lights may be—a healing one.

Mantras are also used in connection with these practices. When you are attempting to reduce someone else's
pain, a mantra can be done silently, in meditation, or both
people may chant it together. The *om mani padme hum* mantra, which is associated in Tibetan symbolism with the Bud-

dha of compassion, is frequently used in healing. For self-healing, the *om ah hum* is recommended.

The same procedure used for healing someone else can be used on yourself. When this is done, you may be able to go much more deeply into the meditation, get into the emotional quality of the green light; this means allowing yourself to welcome its arrival as if it were a being come to help you. When the light is clearly seen and felt, your awareness also flows to the part of yourself where the pain is experienced. The trick in this, as in all Buddhist practices, is not to force something to happen, but to have a sense of openness to the phenomena you are allowing to come into existence.

A SIMPLE but powerful breathing exercise in the Tibetan system is useful either for self-healing or when working with someone else. It is a "deep-roll" breath, somewhat similar to breathing techniques employed in hatha yoga and Reichian therapy. To do it you should be lying comfortably on your back, either on a bed or on a floor with a pad. The precise details of the position are not too important, but since the exercise involves diaphragmmatic breathing, it is usually advisable for people who have not practiced similar exercises to keep one hand lightly on the stomach. The inhalation is in three parts: You begin by raising the belly so that the air flows into the lower part of the lungs. In the second part of the inhalation, which flows smoothly from the first, fill the middle part of the lung cavity, above the stomach. In the final part of the inhalation the upper chest cavity is filled, and there may be a slight raising of the shoulders. Then the breath is slowly and smoothly exhaled, relaxing first the upper chest, then the middle, and finally the lower section of the lungs; you should feel your belly lowering under your hand as the final part of the breath is expelled.

This exercise should ideally be performed for at least twenty minutes, to allow it to do its work. You will find that it tends to bring up feelings, to make you aware of what is

going on in the physical/emotional centers of your being.
Sometimes strong feelings of grief or anger may surface, and
for this reason it can be helpful to have someone else present; sometimes it will put you in touch with areas of physical
tension, and when this happens, massage or self-massage
can be helpful.

The roll breath can be done slowly, for a few minutes,
as a simple relaxation exercise, or it can be done more rapidly, as a way of generating energy. In a time of crisis, when
you feel a buildup of emotions or tension, it can be done
slowly for as long as ninety minutes; as long as you maintain
a comfortable pace, you will not hyperventilate. Basically it
is a clearing process, a way of allowing feelings to come up
and move out, a release for stored blocks in the nervous
system.

CLEARLY there are parts of the Tibetan technology of relaxation and healing that we can learn and use. But we miss
something very important if we look at it only as a set of
practices—some more adaptable than others—to be sorted
out and used. We need to pay attention to the philosophy
that underlies them; I do not mean only the advice about
changing some of our ego-driven and self-destructive ways
of living, although that is in itself of great value. I mean the
Tantric concept of interconnectedness, the ancient mahayana principle of compassion. We will never hear all of
what Tibetan Buddhism has to tell us about health if we let
those meanings slip past us and do not look at the im-
mensely wider context of health to which they draw our
attention.

In recent years there has been a growing interest in holistic health, in the idea that health is not only physical but
emotional, that health practices must be aimed toward
maintaining an optimum state of well-being and not just toward curing isolated diseases. This is a promising development, but the holistic movement is still limited as long as we

continue to think of health in terms of the well-being of individuals; it is not yet holistic, but if we can absorb a bit of Buddhism, we might make it so.

The Tantric concept of interconnectedness becomes less of a mystery when we bring it into our own experience and consider the extent to which our bodies are affected by radiation, carcinogenic substances in the environment, chemicals in the air, in water, and in our food. We can understand this better if we consider that our lungs are connected to countless automobile exhausts, and that people thousands of years in the future are being bequeathed the doubtful karma of today's nuclear generators. Mahayana Buddhism teaches that enlightenment is not to be attained by the individual until everyone is liberated, and—applying this principle to health—it follows that one person cannot be fully healthy until everybody is.

6. The Expanding Universe and the Expanding Mind

I live near a neighborhood of theological seminaries, schools of various denominations that huddle together in ecumenical coziness around a knobby rise known to generations of Berkeley students as Holy Hill. Amid these ivy-covered buildings, students absorb their respective theological heritages and prepare themselves for careers in the ministry. These schools have some minor administrative connections—library privileges and the like—to the publicly supported University of California, a block or so away, but basically they are separate institutions, as befits our separation of church and state.

Western society thrives on separations. I often walk to the top of Holy Hill, which is an admirable place to muse on this subject. From there you can see, on the higher hills, the university's nuclear-research complex: the cyclotron, the central research laboratory, the nuclear-chemistry building. The theology students on Holy Hill do not, of course, have much idea of what goes on in those rather ugly structures; that is not their business. And the nuclear-research people are for the most part no-nonsense scientific rationalists who do not take much interest in theology.

Off to the south of Holy Hill, spread out over hundreds of acres like a map of the compartmentalized Western mind, is the main campus, with all its other separate buildings for separate pursuits of wisdom. One of the closest buildings, from that particular vantage point, is Tolman Hall, the head-quarters of the psychology department. Philosophy, natu-rally, is in another building, some distance away.

Also visible from the top of Holy Hill is the Nyingma Institute, the Tibetan Buddhist meditation center. It sits amid this vast department store of knowledge, its bright prayer flags fluttering in the fresh bay breezes, a curious emissary from another time and place. People of many dif-ferent persuasions and areas of specialization find their way here: theology students from Holy Hill, philosophy students from the university, psychologists and counselors and therapists from all over the San Francisco Bay Area, even an occasional scientist from up on Cyclotron Way. They come and examine Tibetan Buddhism from their various individ-ual perspectives, and decide what it is about. The whole thing is just a little like the old parable of the blind men and the elephant.

THE GREATEST HINDRANCE to our understanding of Ti-betan Buddhism is our habit of compartmentalizing knowl-edge; Western civilization has isolated areas of inquiry from one another in a way that the East has not, so when we want to approach an Eastern subject, we naturally ask first what compartment it belongs in. As soon as we put it in its place, we study it according to our definition of that "subject"—al-ways a Western definition.

Most people naturally categorize Buddhism as a religion, and expect it to behave in the way a modern religion is supposed to behave—to speculate about God, and remove its hat when in the presence of scientific facts.

This causes countless problems, little breakdowns in cross-cultural communication. The Dalai Lama traveled to Europe in 1973 and met with the pope and other religious leaders on the continent and in England. Sometimes they tried to draw him into conversations about God; he pleaded ignorance of the subject. "God is your business," he told one questioner. "Karma is my business."[1]

Some religion, whose leader will not talk about God.

Dimly sensing the unsatisfactoriness of setting Buddhism piously on a shelf alongside the rest of "the world's great religions," Westerners have again and again tried to fit it into other compartments. Some Europeans decided to take it as a stoic nontheistic philosophy, which was fine as long as they confined their attention to early Buddhism, and in fact to very limited parts of that. They could do very little with the occult and erotic material, except disapprove of it.

Alan Watts, whom I have mentioned as one of the great popularizers of Zen in the United States, came to the conclusion that the psychological window was the best one through which to view the wisdom of the East: "If we look deeply into such ways of life . . ." he wrote, "we do not find either philosophy or religion as these are understood in the West. We find something more nearly resembling psychotherapy."[2]

And that, indeed, is the way thousands of Americans have approached Buddhism: as a way of reducing stress, developing awareness, and dealing with the many pains of human existence.

Well, Buddhism *is* a psychotherapy, and on the whole we are making admirable progress in harnessing some of its ancient insights to that peculiarly Western art. But then as soon as we get it comfortably fitted into that category, somebody points a finger in another direction, says, "Look over there," and calls it to our attention that Buddhism is something else entirely.

In the 1970s it was discovered that Buddhism—in fact, the Oriental religions generally—constitutes something akin to what we think of as physics, the study of the material universe. This time the chief finger pointer was a theoretical physicist, Fritjof Capra, a denizen of those bleak buildings in the hills above Berkeley who wrote an eloquent and widely read book entitled *The Tao of Physics* about the parallels between Oriental religions and modern theoretical physics.

Each of these discoveries of a new way to look at Oriental religion is the result of change in our own culture. The basics of Buddhism have not altered over the past few decades, but Western society has passed through—or is in the midst of—any number of intellectual revolutions, explosions in our separate categories of knowledge. Each of these alters our perspective, brings us to a place from which we can take a fresh look at things from outside Western culture.

Our religious traditions, for example, have offered little help or encouragement to the prospective student of Buddhism. But American religion has been undergoing great upheavals, both inside and outside the churches. The most obvious manifestation of this is the "new spirituality," the remarkable turn toward esoteric teachings involving mystery, inner experience, personal transformation, and altered states of consciousness. This has gone well beyond the status of a passing fad, and it has required American theologians to develop a keen interest and a real if cautious openness toward such exotics. As they investigate Buddhism, they discover, somewhat to their relief, that it is not exactly a religion in the Western sense and therefore does not exactly conflict with Western religion.

Psychology has also been going through some changes. There was a time when the word "psychology," in America,

meant either Freudianism or behaviorism—the former the
dominant force in psychotherapy, the latter the dominant
force in academic and theoretical psychology. Neither of
these could spare much time for ideas or practices from the
East: The Freudians were interested in religious symbols
only when they could be hammered into handy psychoanalytic concepts, and the behaviorists were downright hostile
toward anything that smacked of mysticism. The only people holding open a door to the East were the Jungians,
custodians of a small and extremely difficult body of psychological theory. But with the emergence of the "third-
force" humanistic psychologies in the 1960s and 1970s we
obtained a comprehensible body of ideas that were accessible both to Oriental philosophy and to the Western lay
reader; Alan Watts drew upon some of these when he wrote
Psychotherapy East and West,[3] his well-known study of the psychological side of Oriental thought.

And then we come to the new physics. There would be
no exploration of similarities between the physical sciences
and Oriental religions, no *Tao of Physics*, if there had not
been a revolution—indeed, a series of revolutions—in
Western theoretical physics. As long as the West was still
seeing the world through Isaac Newton's eyes, it had no way
at all of making sense of Buddhism as a theory of physics.
But modern physics provides a fundamentally different set
of ideas about the nature of the cosmos, as Capra notes in
the beginning of his book:

> The exploration of the atomic and subatomic world in the
> twentieth century has revealed an unsuspected limitation of
> classical ideas, and has necessitated a radical revision of
> many of our basic concepts. The concept of matter in sub-
> atomic physics, for example, is totally different from the tra-
> ditional idea of a material substance in classical physics. The
> same is true for concepts like space, time, or cause and ef-
> fect. These concepts, however, are fundamental to our out-

look on the world around us and with their radical transformation our whole world-view has begun to change.

These changes . . . all seem to lead in the same direction, toward a view of the world which is very similar to the view held in Eastern mysticism.[4]

To understand what Capra is trying to tell us and see how it relates to Tibetan Buddhism, we need to do two things: first, review some of the basic ideas of Tibetan Buddhism and see how they stand up as statements about the physical universe; second, take a look at our own ideas about physics, both the old and the new.

Buddhist physics is expressed in such themes as impermanence, nonduality, and especially that most mysterious but most central of mahayana concepts, shunyata. Shunyata means not only the "great void" that is the source of all physical objects but also the essential quality of physical objects as well. "That which is form is emptiness," says the Heart Sutra. "That which is emptiness, form."

This concept, the keystone of mahayana philosophy, carried through into vajrayana Buddhism; the diamond—clear yet indestructible, colorless yet capable of reflecting all color—is a symbol for shunyata. Tibetan Buddhism also refined and expanded upon the concept of change, the instability of all events. Then there is the Tantric emphasis upon the interconnectedness of all things, and its curious—to us—refusal to make easy distinctions between matters of the mind and matters of the "real world."

These ideas fit into many boxes: They are moral-philosophical precepts about the futility of becoming attached to any object in a world of insubstantiality and change, religious doctrines about the ultimate nature of reality, psychological concepts about the perception of form, and *physical* statements about matter and energy. As physics, Buddhism is obviously quite different from the Newtonian variety. In

Newton's view God created a universe of physical entities, and ordained fixed laws about how those bodies were to move and function. Here is Newton:

> It seems probable to me that God in the beginning formed matter in solid, massy, hard, impenetrable movable particles, of such sizes and figures, and with such other properties, and in such proportion to space, as most conduced to the end for which he formed them; and that these primitive particles being solids, are incomparably harder than any porous bodies compounded of them; even so very hard, as never to wear or break in pieces; no ordinary power being able to divide what God himself made one in the first creation.[5]

Newton gave us the mechanistic cosmos, the great clockwork of solid bodies moving through space. The solid bodies were composed of solid particles, and, although they might be in motion, they occupied space in the way that A. N. Whitehead has described as "simple location."

> To say that matter has simple location means that ... it is adequate to state that it is where it is, in a definite finite region of space, and throughout a definite finite duration of time, apart from any essential reference of the relations of that bit of matter to other regions of space and to other durations of time. . . .[6]

All of this fits the image of a universe made up of a lot of *things*, things that are out there someplace—separate from us and from one another, capable of being seen and touched, complete unto themselves. This requires a certain way of looking at the universe, and also a certain way of looking at the looker; there must be a clear distinction between subject and object.

We often identify this distinction with Newton's predecessor René Descartes. Descartes, in his *Discourse on Method* and in *Principles*, worked out a set of basic concepts for understanding the physical universe, with a radical separation of the "I," the knower of phenomena, from the world of observed phenomena. Actually, there were three elements in Descartes' system: the I, the world, and God; but God was rather remote from the center of Cartesian philosophy. The main categories were the *res cogitans* of thought and the *res extensa* of physical objects. Everything had to be one or the other, and a surprisingly large portion of the universe ended up in the latter category. Not only inanimate objects but plants and animals were classed as unthinking machinery.

Descartes provided the intellectual basis for modern science: a universe of bodies moving through space according to mechanistic laws, and a separate human intelligence capable of observing their behavior and discovering the laws. Descartes' concepts aided Newton's magnificent research on the movement and gravitation of bodies.

This development marked a move away from older, organismic concepts of the universe, in which matter was thought to be interconnected and alive. Organismic similes sometimes turned up in Newton's writings, but we can see now that a new and different world view was being created. In this view the universe was a collection of discrete objects, any one of which could be looked at separately and analyzed separately. And the creative, moving intelligence, God, was no longer busily present in all its functions. Descartes and Newton both included God in their philosophies, but whether they knew it or not, they were getting the world ready to separate science from theology, digging the gulch between Holy Hill and the laboratories. God for Descartes was the least significant part of his triangular view of the cosmos, an abstract point of reference: It would be easy for later philosophers of science to talk merely about the observer and the thing observed. Similarly, Newton's God seemed to have retired from the scene once he had done the work of creating the laws and setting the universe in motion. It would be easy for Newton's followers to continue the work of studying the clock and to declare the clockmaker to be somebody else's department.

Classical physics led to spectacular breakthroughs in scientific inquiry and technology, and spurred one of the most optimistic and enthusiastic periods in all human history. It seemed as though the human mind was now capable of comprehending nature's innermost secrets through the rigorous application of scientific method. The poet Alexander Pope, catching the exuberant spirit of the times, wrote:

> Nature and Nature's laws lay hid in night:
> Then God said, Let Newton be! and all was light!

But, as we are now beginning to understand, each proud breakthrough into an expanded understanding of the natural world is only a partial and transient victory; new discoveries fit together into a new reality that turns out to be as fragile as the old. Human progress is like that of a mountain climber who thinks he sees the top of the mountain, only to get there and discover it was only a rise and that he still had a way to go. Thomas Kuhn, in his classic work *The Structure of Scientific Revolutions*, has shown what happens to scientific paradigms; in each field a new theory emerges and reigns for a while as the official reality until its foundations begin to crack and it finally crumbles and is replaced by the next official reality.[7] In many cases scientific theories profoundly influence the entire culture, so that a scientific revolution is a world-shattering event that changes our entire conception of humanity and the cosmos. Such was the case with the Copernican revolution in astronomy, and the Darwinian revolution in natural science.

Newtonian physics reverberated through the Western world, became a major influence on the French Enlightenment, inspired political philosophers such as Locke and Voltaire, and launched the new technologies of the Industrial Revolution. For more than a century Newton's ideas stood as the official reality, and then the cracks began to show.

In 1887 a pair of American scientists, A. A. Michelson and E. W. Morley, conducted an experiment in measuring the speed of light; conceived entirely within the Newtonian paradigm and carried out with exquisite precision, the experiment was supposed to reveal minor differences in the speed of light as it traveled in different directions relative to the earth's orbit. The experimenters found no differences. Light was not behaving as Newtonian mechanics said it should.

In 1905 Albert Einstein published his paper on the special theory of relativity, the first step toward the creation of a non-Newtonian paradigm, a new conception of space and time in which there was no longer any "simple location" or absolute time.[8] A body could not be merely "there," either in rest or in motion, but only in relation to other bodies; time had no meaning save in relation to space, nor space save in relation to time. In his famous equation $E = mc^2$ Einstein proclaimed that mass is really a form of energy, that all matter is made up not of indivisible small particles, as Newton had supposed, but of vibrating patterns of something— or nothing—that could manifest itself as either energy or matter. Research in atomic physics proceeded to give a more exact yet somehow elusive picture of the nature of these patterns, and the atomic bomb showed the world that the atom was indeed divisible, and that mass could be converted into awesome energy. Well before that spectacular development, the Newtonian paradigm had already lost its hold on theoretical physics. Capra writes:

> The first three decades of our century changed the whole situation in physics radically. Two separate developments— that of relativity theory and of atomic physics—shattered all the principal concepts of the Newtonian world view: the notion of absolute space and time, the elementary solid parti-

cles, the strictly causal nature of physical phenomena, and
the ideal of an objective description of nature. None of these
concepts could be extended to the new domain into which
physics was now moving.[9]

The new domain into which physics was moving
seemed to be less and less concerned with *things;* it was, like
the cosmos of Buddhism, a domain of *events:*

> . . . in the quantum view, the motion of material entities hav-
> ing form, a discrete and fixed special configuration, and en-
> durance, a continuous sustenance through time, yields to the
> notion of process, a dynamical act of continuously evolving
> *becoming.* . . . Apart from process, there is no being. . . . Its re-
> ality is defined by the unity of the various processes which
> enter into its make-up.[10]

What had happened? A hundred years ago, science, still
standing with its feet steady on the Newtonian paradigm,
had aspired to discover the nature of the atom, the ultimate
building block of solid matter. When science finally came to
the atom and penetrated it, a whole new world of subatomic
particles opened up before its vision. As those subatomic
particles were studied, it became clear that whatever they
were, they were not simply little chunks of solid stuff.
Sometimes they could be described as particles, sometimes
as waves. You could never precisely say that they were
"there" but could only venture that they had a tendency to
be there. The probability would be affected by what you did
to determine whether they were there or not. Sometimes
they seemed to appear from nowhere and disappear back
into it. To say that things emanate from the void sounds
strange and Oriental. But put into "science talk" it only
sounds strange:

> . . . quantum electrodynamics reveals that an electron, posi-
> tron and photon occasionally emerge spontaneously from a
> perfect vacuum. When this happens, the three particles exist

for a brief time, and then annihilate each other, leaving no trace behind. (Energy conservation is violated, but only for the brief particle lifetime. . . .) The spontaneous temporary emergence of particles from a vacuum is called vacuum fluctuation, and is utterly commonplace in quantum field theory.[11]

As physics went further and further into the atom, it passed through the Newtonian paradigm, like Alice walking through the mirror, and emerged into a world in which there were vast empty spaces, and fleeting events that could only with great charity be described as "things": shunyata, emanation from the void; and impermanence:

> . . . the empirical evidence available thus far shows that nothing has yet been discovered which has a mode of being that remains eternally defined in any given way. Rather, every element, however fundamental it may seem to be, has always been found under suitable conditions to change even in its basic qualities, and to become something else. . . . The notion of something with an exhaustively specifiable and unvarying mode of being can only be an approximation and an abstraction from the infinite complexity of the changes taking place in the real process of becoming.[12]

In this breathtaking new view of reality even that most durable foundation stone of classical physics, the subject-object distinction, was found to be obsolete.

A famous scientific concept concerning this issue is Werner Heisenberg's "principle of uncertainty," which was developed out of the attempt to study and measure the behavior of subatomic particles. Heisenberg and other scientists discovered that every attempt to observe such particles had some sort of an effect on them. There was no longer any such thing as a world of natural phenomena "out there" that one could simply look at objectively; nor was there a separate and supremely detached observer. Down in the mysterious depths of the atom, as the apparatus of observation intersected with subatomic events, the boundary between *res cogitans* and *res extensa* simply ceased to exist. And scientists began to wonder if it had ever really existed at all, except, as in other parts of the world view of classical physics, as a productive way of dealing with certain limited data. Heisenberg himself was convinced that research in subatomic physics had led to a new conceptualization of science.

> We cannot disregard the fact that natural science is formed by men. Natural science does not simply describe and explain nature; it is a part of the interplay between nature and ourselves; it describes nature as exposed to our mode of questioning. This was a possibility of which Descartes could not have thought, but it makes the sharp separation between the world and the I impossible.[13]

While the physicists were revising their view of the universe through discoveries at the subatomic level, the astronomers were encountering equally strange goings-on out among the galaxies. In 1913 an astronomer in Arizona, V. M. Sipher, discovered the phenomenon called the "red shift," which indicated that about a dozen galaxies in the earth's vicinity were not staying in their places but were flying away from us at enormous speeds. An expanding universe: an awesome, mind-boggling discovery, and another blow to the Newtonian image of an orderly cosmos.

So paradigms changed in physics and astronomy; scientists came to different ways of looking at things; the old physics gave way to the new. But note something very curious here: There have been a number of revolutions in science, yet the old physics is still with us. Our everyday consciousness still dwells in the world of subjects and objects, hard bodies, and simple location—or thinks it does. We do not, in fact, know how to experience the physical universe that our scientists have discovered; I am not at all sure that the scientists who have discovered it feel particularly at home there either. We seem to have accepted a perpetual split between the world of ordinary human experience and the incomprehensible truths of modern science. We read in the paper every few months that science has just pulled the props out from some other fundamental principle with which we used to structure reality; we are awed by the news and yet unchanged by it; with each discovery the cosmos expands, but we do not. It is out there, and we are in here.

As soon as we take note of this peculiar position we are in, really appreciate its strangeness, we are in a much better place to understand Tibetan Buddhism.

The vajrayana is a religious path oriented toward developing people who are capable of experiencing a non-Newtonian, non-Cartesian reality, consciously and purposefully living in such a universe. After all, philosophical notions of an organismic cosmos, of insubstantiality and change and nonduality, are not in themselves unique to Buddhism. Many philosophers, East and West, have seen the world in such terms. Buddhism's uniqueness is in being a humanistic, experiential system, one with a deep concern about the predicament of being human in the universe, and with a technology for experiencing what its philosophy describes.

Buddhism presents a way of looking at the cosmos, and says that we do not know how to live in it. Not understanding its true nature, we make ourselves miserable trying to stand apart from it and deal with it as a bunch of solid objects, some of which we might with luck be able to grasp and hold on to for a while. The Buddhist cosmos, as depicted in the Surangama Sutra, is made up of parts that deny their connection to the whole:

> In my practice of Dhyana I . . . reflected on how the great world was upheld in space, on how the great world was kept in perpetual motion, on how my body was kept in motion, and maintained by breathing, upon the movement of the

mind, thoughts rising and passing. I reflected upon these various things and marvelled at their great sameness without any difference save in the rate of vibration. I realized that the nature of these vibrations had neither any source for their coming, nor destination for their going, and that all sentient beings, as numerous as the infinitesimal particles of dust in vast spaces, were each in his own way topsy-turvy balanced by vibrations, and that each and every one was obsessed with the illusion that he was a unique creation.[14]

This is the human plight that Buddhism addresses itself to, the existential unsatisfactoriness described in the first noble truth. And the way out that Buddhism offers is to become free through understanding the situation; the Buddhist scriptures speak of achieving liberation through perceiving the identity of form and emptiness. The ego-centered, samsaric mind is one separated from reality and trapped miserably in a world of objects. Liberation is freedom from attachment, after all, and how can you be attached to anything when you correctly perceive that in the universe there are only events in flux?

Tibetan Buddhist practices are designed to reflect that reality into the deepest recesses of the mind; its mysterious gimmickry of mantras and breathing exercises is intended to develop a finely tuned human organism capable of experiencing flowing energy and eternal change.

The extinction of ego, that spiritual goal that has so often been mistakenly equated, in both the East and the West, with self-abnegation or unconsciousness, is better understood as a state of being fully awake and aware. Nirvana is freedom from ideas of permanence or solidity, with no split between the knower and the known. The enlightened mind understands that it participates actively in all the events the samsaric mind takes to be objective, eternal reality.

Buddhist writings repeatedly speak of the illusory quality of life. The world is compared to a magic show, to a dream, to images reflected in a mirror. This does not mean, as many people believe, that Buddhism says that everything is in your mind and the world is just something you make up. True, Buddhism did produce schools of thought that came close to what is known in Western philosophy as "mentalism" or "idealism." The most influential were the Yogacaras, whose doctrine was "mind only." But the mainstream of Buddhist thought, and certainly of Tibetan Buddhist thought, is a more subtle and relativistic understanding. "For one of superior intellect," says one Tibetan text, "the best thing is to have thorough comprehension of the inseparableness of the knower, the object of knowledge, and the act of knowing."[15] Longchenpa rejects complete mentalism in favor of an image of the universe based on three "potentialities for experience," which are body, consciousness, and objects; although these can be conceptualized separately, they have no existence apart from one another.[16]

In the Tibetan view the cosmos is not "made up" in your mind. Mind interpenetrates the cosmos, is inseparable from it, is as truly a dimension as are time and space in Newtonian physics. "There is no such thing as internal or external," says Longchenpa.[17]

The shift of consciousness that Buddhist practice seeks to achieve is a matter of adjusting one's sensitivities and intelligence toward a different understanding—something akin to learning one's way around a new neighborhood or comprehending a difficult piece of scientific theory—but it is more than a merely intellectual development. In Buddhist tradition it is also personal growth and spiritual development. Recall that the mahayana linked the understanding of "no-thing-ness" with the awakening of compassion. Buddhists often talk of the changes in *character* that accompany a comprehension of the truth of shunyata.[18] In *The Dawn of Tantra*, written with Herbert V. Guenther, Chögyam Trungpa proceeds from a technical discussion of shunyata meditative practices to a description of the results. He says, "This experience produces a new dimension—one finds one doesn't have to defend oneself any longer. The experience of shunyata brings a sense of independence, a sense of freedom."[19] Later he takes this a step further:

> Shunyata is clearly not a state of trance or an absorption of some kind. It is a fearless state. Because of this fearlessness, one can afford to be generous. One can afford to acknowledge a space which does not contain any conflicts of that and this or how and why. No questions of any kind exist at this point. But within this state there is a tremendous sense of freedom. It is an experience, I suppose one could say, of having gone beyond. But this does not mean that one has gone beyond in the sense of having abandoned "here" and therefore having gotten beyond to "there." Rather it's that one is here, or one is there, *already.*   So a tremendous sense of conviction begins to develop with the shunyata experience. Shunyata provides the basic inspiration for developing the ideal, so to speak, of bodhisattva-like behavior.[20]

It is the *experience* of shunyata, then, not just the concept, that is so central to Buddhist teaching. Buddhism is an integrated statement about the nature of the cosmos, the situation of being human in it, and the way of dealing with the problem. No part of it can really be taken separately, and no other system of thought has put together anything quite comparable to the Buddhist perspective; it is not surprising that it has endured for 2500 years.

One of the remarkable things about Buddhism is that it does not have much to say about how things got to be the way they are. We could speculate that it was an inevitable evolutionary development, that the struggle for survival necessitated the development of an intelligence pervaded with notions of concreteness and ego, but that would be, for a true Buddhist, an empty intellectual digression and no help in dealing with the problem at hand. The Buddhist scriptures merely say that something went wrong: "Listen! From the motive force for well-being, conceptual fictions and unstable actions miraculously appear."[21]

And so we live cut off from our true nature, steeped in the error the philosophers call the "fallacy of misplaced concreteness."

The Newtonian universe seems to be an attractive, somehow comfortable, however erroneous, place to inhabit. It is a world of familiar dimensions and solid pieces of furniture. Why should we embrace that other reality the scientists talk about, in which all is motion and energy, in which the solid little bits of matter turn out to be vibrating empty spaces and the gigantic galaxies spin away from us at a million miles an hour? A scientist would shrug and say that that's the universe we inhabit, whether we acknowledge it or not. A Tibetan Buddhist, putting the same information into terms most of us find infuriatingly obscure, would say that ordinary mind and enlightened mind, samsara and nirvana, are really the same thing. Buddhism insists that the feeling of solidity and permanence is not really all that comfortable, because it is an illusion. Chögyam Trungpa says:

> To realize impermanence is to realize that death is taking place constantly and birth is taking place constantly; so there really is nothing fixed. If one begins to realize this and does not push against the natural course of events, it is no longer necessary to re-create samsara at every moment. Samsara, or the samsaric mentality, is based on solidifying your existence, making yourself permanent, everlasting. In order to do that, since there actually is nothing to grasp or hold onto or sit on, you have to re-create the grasping, the perching, the speeding constantly.[22]

To Buddhism the familiar world of objects and egos, however homey it might appear, is a trap; and the wide-open spaces of shunyata, however strange they might seem, are the realm of freedom.

SOONER OR LATER, I suspect, our various philosophical and scientific revolutions will cease to be separate explosions in separate compartments, and will end up destroying the partitions that fence off our minds and lives. To some extent this is happening already: The new spiritualism and the new psychologies overlap at so many points that they sometimes seem to be one movement. Ministers sermonize freely about self-actualization, and churches offer group therapy, and "third-force" humanistic psychology has produced "fourth-force" transpersonal psychology, with its own professional association and scholarly journal full of articles about such things as meditation and brain-wave research.

Could there ever be a similar coming-together of psychology and physics? A rather far-out thought, but you will hear it expressed in highly respectable circles. Speaking from the discipline of neurophysiological research, Karl Pribram theorizes that "we perceive a physical universe not much different in basic organization from the brain," and is seeking to discover the details of that universal structure.[23] David Bohm, in physics, has come to the parallel conclusion that "the real material of theoretical physics is the nature of thought."[24]

So, as we probe the mind and the universe, we revise our understanding of both, and begin to suspect they are not separate after all. And the scientific West sails ever closer to the mysterious East.

7. Dream Analysis, Tibetan Style

I n dreams the strangeness of life is most inescapable;
even those of us who have the waking hours all figured
out and under control find ourselves nightly drifting
through a terrain of mystery and sometimes terror, where
forms change and meanings elude us. Dreams have fascinated mystics and philosophers and poets for centuries, and
the subject is still as fascinating, and as incomprehensible, as
it ever was. There is scarcely a single piece of information
about dreaming that is universally accepted by all the "au-
thorities" on the subject.

This rich terrain is currently being trampled through by
seekers of all descriptions who suspect it must contain valu-
able clues about the nature of human life. Philosophers are
trying to analyze the content of dreams; scientists are hook-
ing people up to machinery to measure its outer physical
manifestations; therapists and spiritual practitioners of various kinds are trying to understand how we can *use* dreams in
our waking lives. Amid this activity you can find almost any

position or interpretation you like. There are people who think that dreams are merely a sort of mental twitch with scarcely any meaning or value at all; there are others who see them as a necessary psychological process, even as a key to the subconscious, the future, inner peace, mental health, or superconsciousness. In some quarters the enthusiasm for dreams runs so high that you are inclined to wonder why anybody would ever want to wake up.

It is hard to believe that anything particularly different could be interjected into this ferment of activity, but, surprisingly, Tibetan Buddhism does bring to the subject of dreams a perspective that I have not encountered anywhere else, except perhaps in the works of Carlos Castaneda. In its perspective on the subject of dreaming, as in other areas, Tibetan Buddhism runs roughly parallel to certain Western notions and then takes off in a direction all its own, into what is at the same time one of the most unusual and most easily sampled methods of spiritual practice, the dream yoga.

In order to get ourselves ready to venture into the Tibetan offering on the subject of dreams, let us take a brief tour through a couple of the central issues that have arisen in Western investigations: the meaning of dreams, and the question of their reality.

People in most civilizations, from the earliest recorded times, believed that dreams had meaning, that they were not simply an incoherent jumble of mental images but rather the source of some kind of *information* that could be of value if properly understood. Dreams were seen as an entrée to the world of the supernatural in which the dreamer made contact with gods and demons who could foresee the future; dreams were symbolic prophecies of future events. In the Bible, for example, the pharaoh dreamed of standing by the river and seeing seven fat cattle emerge from it, followed by seven lean cattle that consumed the seven fat ones; this was interpreted by Joseph as a portent of seven years of plenty followed by seven years of famine. The dream became the basis of the pharaoh's policy of laying up stores for the future during the seven prosperous years, and was also the cause of Joseph's rise to a position of power as adviser to the pharaoh. It is important to note that in the Biblical account Joseph explicitly described the dream as a direct revelation from God.[1]

Aristotle was one of the first to argue that dreams were not of divine origin but rather a manifestation in the psyche of the dreamer; this did not entirely separate dreams from the realm of the supernatural, since for Aristotle the human spirit had a natural kinship with the divine. But his ideas on the subject were definitely tending in the direction of a more secular view of dreaming.[2]

Although various philosophers after Aristotle raised the idea that dreaming was not an exclusively supernatural phenomena, it remained the popular belief, until well into this century, that dreams could foretell future events. "Dream books" showing how to interpret dreams were widely consulted.

When scientists began to study dreams and sleep, they were skeptical of the idea that dreams had prophetic content, and as this traditional notion was debunked, dreams were left without any meaning at all. Science was increasingly inclined to view them in mechanistic terms, as something the brain did, either in responding to somatic stimuli or in randomly reprocessing the events of the dreamer's waking hours. Your choice was to believe in dreams as prophecy or to dismiss them as a meaningless lower order of brain functioning.

Into the midst of this division rode Sigmund Freud, with his famous dictum that dreams were "the royal road to the unconscious." Yes, said Freud, dreams can be interpreted; they can be *scientifically* interpreted by the psychoanalyst so as to reveal the repressed underside of the human psyche. The dream, Freud said, is a device whereby the psyche fulfills its wishes, acts out things the dreamer wants to do or say or feel but cannot, because of the repressive force of the socially conditioned conscience, or superego. The dream allows something forbidden to be experienced, but also censors that by changing the dream content into symbols. "We should then assume," Freud wrote, "that in every human being there exist, as the primary cause of dream-formation, two psychic forces . . . one of which forms the wish expressed by the dream, while the other exercises a censorship over this dream-wish, thereby enforcing on it a distortion."[3] And, since Freud was convinced that repression mainly concerned sexuality, his analysis of dreams dealt largely with the sexual content of dream images. So dream interpretation lost its status as prophecy and supernatural experience, and entered the era of the phallic symbol.

Other schools of psychology and therapy have followed Freud's basic proposition that dreams have a discoverable and useful psychological content, without going all the way with his theory that they are the disguised expression of repressed wishes. Carl Jung doubted that a dreamer deliberately conceals the dream's true meaning.

> I was never able to agree with Freud that the dream is a "facade" behind which its meaning lies hidden—a meaning already known but maliciously, so to speak, withheld from consciousness. To me dreams are a part of nature, which harbors no intention to deceive, but expresses something as best it can, just as a plant grows or an animal seeks its food as best it can. These forms of life, too, have no wish to deceive our eyes, but we may deceive ourselves because our eyes are shortsighted.[4]

For Jung, who of all modern psychological theorists was most conversant with the esoteric teachings of the East, the interpretation of dreams requires an understanding first of the "collective unconscious" and, second, of "archetypes."

In Jung's psychology there is a level of mental activity at which thinking is no longer personal but transpersonal, nonindividual. "The collective unconscious is common to all," he said. "It is the foundation of what the ancients called the 'sympathy of all things.' "[5] Since this collective unconscious sometimes manifests itself in dreams, Jung considered it entirely possible for dreams to involve experiences of extrasensory perception—knowledge of events happening elsewhere or contact with the thoughts of others.

Jung's concept of "archetypes" was his contribution to the quest for the fundamental structures of human consciousness, the forms we use to make the world meaningful. "The concept of the archetype," he said, ". . . is derived from the repeated observation that, for instance, the myths and fairy-tales of world literature contain definite motifs which crop up everywhere. We meet these same motifs in fantasies, dreams, deliria, and delusions of individuals living today. These typical images and associations are what I call archetypal ideas."[6] The concept of the archetype gave Jung a greatly expanded frame of reference in looking for the meaning of dreams; dream symbols might express the deepest mythic or religious forms of the human consciousness.

Gestalt therapy is still another system that starts from the basic Freudian conviction that dreams express a psychological meaning. But Gestalt "dreamwork" also comes close to Buddhism in some respects. For example, Fritz Perls insisted that the content of dreams should not be fragmented into a subject-object model of experience. Everything in the dream had to be recognized and assimilated as a part of the dreamer. And there is another similarity: Gestalt dreamwork, like Tibetan dream yoga, is more experiential than analytic.

The method of Gestalt dreamwork is a modified form of psychodrama: The subject gives an oral summary of the dream, is asked to narrate the dream in the present tense, and is then encouraged to act out the parts of the various dream images. Out of this kind of work come sessions such as the following: A woman tells of a dream in which she saw a lake drying up, while a circle of porpoises, about to die, stood sadly in a circle on a small island. There should have been a treasure at the bottom of the lake, the woman says, but all she could see was an old license plate. The dream session proceeds:

PERLS: Will you please play this license plate.

C. [the woman]: I am an old license plate, thrown in the bottom of a lake. I have no use because I'm of no value. I'm not rusted, I'm outdated. So, I can't be used. I'm just thrown on the rubbish heap. . . . The use of the license plate is to allow—to give a car permission to go—and I can't give anyone permission to do anything because I'm outdated. In California they just paste a little—you buy a sticker and stick it on the car—on the old license plates. So, maybe someone would put me on their car and stick a new sticker on me. I don't . . .

PERLS: OK. Play now the lake.

C.: I am a lake. I am drying up and disappearing—soaking into the earth—dying. But, when I soak into the earth and become part of the earth, maybe I water the surrounding area, so—even the lake—even in my bed—flowers can grow. New life can grow (starting to cry) from me—

PERLS: Do you get the existential message?

C.: Yes. I can—I can create. I can create beauty—but I can no longer reproduce. I'm like the porpoise—I'm . . . But, I—I keep wanting to say, "food." I—as water, become—I *water* the earth and give life—growing things. The water—they need both the earth and the water—and the air and sun. But, as the water and the lake, I can play a part.

PERLS: You see the contrast—on the surface you find some *thing*, some artifact—the license plate—the artificial you. But when you go deeper, you find the apparent *death* of the lake is actually fertility.

C.: I don't really need this plate—or permission—or a license plate in order to—

PERLS: Nature doesn't need a license plate to grow.[7]

Perls frequently described dreams as "existential messages," meanings or feelings struggling to be understood and accepted. Gestalt dreamwork has its analytic side, as the above passage shows, but the patient plays an active part in it. The meanings are not required to conform to any predetermined ideology; the process itself—the work of integrating the dream meaning into the waking life—is the essence of the therapy.

THEN there is the matter of the relationship between dream reality and waking reality. In dreams we have experiences that seem real to us at the time, and then, upon awakening, we immediately assume that everything that has gone before was an illusion and we are now in the world of reality. Most of us make that assumption, but many people at one time or another have questioned it—wondered if perhaps the dream state is real also, or the waking state really another kind of dream.

> Once Chuang Chou dreamed that he was a butterfly. He fluttered about happily, quite pleased with the state he was in, and knew nothing about Chuang Chuo. Presently he awoke and found that he was very much Chuang Chou again. Now, did Chou dream that he was a butterfly or was the butterfly now dreaming that he was Chou?[8]

The above passage is from a Chinese text dated about 300 B.C.; apparently people have been wondering about dreams and reality for a long, long time.

One of the classic discussions of this issue was penned by René Descartes, and since I have already reincarnated him once in this book, we may as well bring him to life again; his thinking has been the center of a heated argument

among contemporary philosophers, and it gives us a particularly good entrée into Tibetan dream yoga.

Descartes was interested in how one could be really
certain of the reality of ordinary sense perceptions. The experience of dreaming inspired him to wonder about this. He
wrote:

> At this moment it does indeed seem to me that it is with eyes
> awake that I am looking at this paper; that this head which I
> move is not asleep, that it is deliberately and of set purpose
> that I extend my hand and perceive it; what happens in sleep
> does not appear so clear nor so distinct as does all this. But in
> thinking over this I remind myself that on many occasions I
> have in sleep been deceived by similar illusions, and in
> dwelling carefully on this reflection I see so manifestly that
> there are no certain indications by which we may clearly
> distinguish wakefulness from sleep that I am lost in aston-
> ishment. And my astonishment is such that it is almost capa-
> ble of persuading me that I now dream.[9]

This is a remarkable statement to come from the same
person who contributed so much to the ground rules of
classical scientific objectivity. For a moment one of the leading minds of Western philosophy stood at the doorway of
the Oriental view of the world; he peeked in, drew back, and
did not enter.

The experience that Descartes relates did not shake his
conviction that there is a world of physical goings-on that is
fundamentally separate from "mind." But it made him
skeptical, unsure of the ability of his senses to report accurately on what was out there: "All that up to the present time
I have accepted as most true and certain," he said, "I have
learned either from the senses or through the senses; but it
is sometimes proved to me that these senses are deceptive,
and it is wiser not to trust entirely to any thing by which we
have once been deceived."[10] The chief legacies of Cartesian
skepticism are the insistence that scientific experiments be

capable of being "replicated"—carried out by other experimenters under precisely the same conditions and with precisely the same results—and the search for more precise, nonhuman technologies of observation and measurement, so that the effects of human fallibility are reduced to the absolute minimum.

Over the past twenty years or so professional philosophers have again taken an interest in the subject of dreaming. Most of this has been in response to Norman Malcolm's essay entitled "Dreaming and Skepticism."[11] The essence of Professor Malcolm's argument is that you can't really use the experience of dreaming as a basis for being skeptical about your waking experience, because it is impossible to prove the truth of any dream. You can't wake somebody up while he or she is dreaming and get an account of what is happening, because that of course stops the dream. All you really get is the form of communication called "telling a dream," which is a different matter, and done only by people who are awake. It is dreams that we should be skeptical about, and not our waking experience.

Malcolm was not out to refute the proposition that there is such a thing as dreaming at all, he was more interested in challenging the logic of Descartes' statement about being deceived in a dream. But other writers have gone so far as to argue that we don't really know at all that we have dreams while we are asleep; perhaps the experiences that we have while asleep—rapid eye movement and all that—are only preparations for a waking experience in which we conjure up fantasy images that we identify as memories of a dream.

These skeptical arguments have something in common with the psychoanalytic and Gestalt approaches to dreams which share the belief that the most important part of the use of dreams in psychotherapy is what happens when the patient is *awake*. The therapeutic breakthrough occurs when the patient understands the dream and integrates it into his or her conscious life. Especially in Gestalt, with its emphasis on staying in the here and now, it is not particularly important to establish that the dream really took place as reported; what is important is the waking experience of "owning" some previously repressed feeling. It is not too far from this to the fantasy or daydream techniques used in some forms of therapy in which the patient—sometimes with the therapist's guidance, sometimes working as part of a group—deliberately goes into a waking dream and carries it through to some satisfactory conclusion. In any such approaches the real concern is with what is happening now, in the waking consciousness.

And in Buddhist psychology the "now" is really all there is. In this instant, this brief pulsation out of the void, there comes together a unique combination of mental events that contains your conception of your self and all the images that you identify as memories. So from the Buddhist point of view it is not particularly necessary to prove or disprove that you really dreamed what you think you did; it is only necessary to work with your present awareness, whether you happen to be asleep or awake.

The goal of the Tibetan way of working with dreams is not to "interpret" them (although it is perfectly all right to do that) but to move to a higher and more awakened state of being, even when you are asleep.

Tibetan dream yoga begins with the proposition that since we dream, we might as well make the most of it. And this means making the most of it while it is happening. Dreams are a slightly different mode of experience, in which, say the Tibetan teachings, the body and mind are functioning in a different way: The dream state has its own chemistry, its own subtle physical system, its own glands that do not function while the body is awake. In the dream state there is a greater spontaneity and flow of experience, an absence of pressure and programming, although the advanced practitioner can, it is said, plan his or her own dreams before going to sleep. In dreams you can explore different ways of being, and you can change.

In order to work (or play) creatively with the dream state and fully explore its possibilities, you must develop a certain awareness while dreaming; the texts speak of "recognizing" dreams, of being aware that you are dreaming without waking up. Having learned how to do this fairly consistently, you can then begin to go further in exploring all the possibilities of dream experience. You can try remembering things that happened while you were awake, or remembering past dreams. You can also try interpreting your dreams while you are having them.

Many people—perhaps all of us—have spontaneous dream-recognition experiences at some time or another. Such experiences are commonly reported in psychological studies of dreams. Charles Tart, in his book on altered states of consciousness, calls them "lucid dreams." The lucid dream, he says, "has the unusual characteristic that the dreamer 'wakes' from an ordinary dream in that he feels he is suddenly in possession of his normal waking consciousness and knows that he is actually lying in bed asleep; *but*, the dream world he is in remains perfectly real."[12]

The next step after you have learned to recognize dreams is to begin to direct them while dreaming. It is suggested that you can try transforming the objects in dreams into other objects, as sorcerers do in fairy tales, and also transform yourself into an animal, another person, an inanimate object.[13] You can also learn to "rewrite" your dream scripts while they are unfolding, and carry the events in your dream life toward more satisfactory conclusions. You can meditate while dreaming, and you can also enter into altered states of consciousness; this might seem to be a contradiction in terms if you define dreaming as something opposite of consciousness, but there are many accounts of people who, in dreams, enter into exhalted states of awareness— "peak" dream experiences qualitatively different from normal waking or sleeping. Historically these have usually been described as "visions" and categorized as religious experiences; among contemporary Americans such experiences are frequently compared to those induced by chemicals. Tart, in the paper in which he discusses the "lucid dream," also talks about the "high dream," which he defines as "an experience occurring during sleep in which you find yourself in another world, the dream world, *and* in which you recognize *during* the dream that you are in an altered state of consciousness, which is similar to (but not necessarily identical with) the high induced by a chemical psychedelic." This is not simply a matter of dreaming that you are taking a drug; rather you actually experience mental processes similar to those induced by the drug. This appears to be a fairly common experience among people who have had some experience with psychedelic drugs; it is not particularly well understood—*nothing* about dreaming is particularly well understood—but it appears that drug experiences either teach people how to get into certain states of consciousness that can be reached more easily when asleep than when awake, or give people a map that enables them to recognize and remember experiences we all have in dreams. There is some evidence, also, that "high dream" experiences can carry through into the waking state, as in the following account:

> I dreamed I got high on some sort of gaseous substance, like LSD in gas form. Space took on an expanded, high quality, my body (dream body) was filled with a delicious sensation of warmth, my mind "high" in an obvious but indescribable way. It only lasted a minute and then I was awakened by one of the kids calling out and my wife getting up to see what was the matter. Then the most amazing thing happened. I stayed high even though awake! It had a sleepy quality to it but the expanded and warm quality of time and space carried over into my perception of the (dimly lit) room. It stayed this way for a couple of minutes, amazing me at the time because I was clearly high, as well as recalling my high dream.[14]

The practice of dream yoga is to enable you to learn how to enter altered states while asleep, and it is also taught that extrasensory experiences can be achieved while sleeping: The sleeper can enter the minds of others, and can become more open to telepathic messages from other people. Some teachings mention the dream state as an opportunity to receive spiritual instructions that you might resist or misunderstand when awake.

There is some scientific evidence to support the hypothesis that ESP potential is heightened during sleep. Stanley Krippner and his associates at the Dream Laboratory of Maimonides Medical Center in New York performed a series of experiments in which "senders" visualized randomly selected art prints, attempting to communicate them to subjects who were asleep in different rooms. The subjects, upon awakening, would be asked to go through the entire set of prints and select those that most closely resembled images they remembered from their dreams. These experiments produced statistically significant results.[15] In a few cases, subjects were spectacularly successful in sketching remembered dream images similar to the prints that had been "projected" by the sender.

In the psychological literature on dreaming you will find all manner of dream experiences recorded, and also a number of practical methods aimed at enhancing the ability of the dreamer to remember dreams; many therapists, for example, encourage their patients to keep a note pad handy by the bedside to write down dream experiences immediately upon awakening, or to make daily entries in a dream journal. However, Western work in dreaming offers very little in the way of specific methods for becoming more aware of dreams while dreaming, or even much consideration of the possibility that it can be done. This is where the Tibetan Buddhist approach brings a unique contribution to the subject; it offers a technology, a body of practices for developing a heightened awareness of dream experiences.

Basically the dream yoga is an extension of the practice of mindfulness in the waking state. If mindfulness practice is observed regularly when awake, it should be easier to improve the quality of your awareness in dreams.

The Tibetan instructions on dream yoga mention some fairly obvious things to be avoided—such as overeating or strenuous exercise at bedtime—and discuss the times when it is easiest to practice:

> The best time to observe dreams is between dawn and sunrise, because this is when food has been digested and rest completed, drowsiness is not heavy, and the mind is comparatively clear. But those who only sleep lightly can also practice this during the night.
>
> The yogi should use a thin quilt, a high pillow, and lie on his side. Before falling asleep, he should strengthen his confidence and determination to recognize dreams at least seven or as many as twenty-one times. . . .
>
> A long and continuous sleep should be avoided; instead, one should try to sleep for many short periods. Each time one wakes up he should review whether he has successfully recognized his dreams during the preceding sleep.[16]

There are also specific meditations, usually involving the throat or heart chakras, to be used prior to going to sleep as an aid to dream recognition. The meditation that I was taught for this purpose was to visualize in the throat an eight-petaled rose with a white light in the center of it. Other practices are more complex, with additional elements in the meditation. A fairly simple presleep meditation, given in the above text, is to visualize a red *om* in the throat chakra, or to intone, in your mind, a long *om* with each breath. Like the other visualization-meditations in vajrayana Buddhism, these require some practice, both in visualization generally and in learning to master whatever specific technique is being used.

So far we have dealt with one part of the dream yoga—

the part that involves what you do while dreaming or getting ready to sleep. There is also a dream yoga that is practiced while you are awake.

The sleeping part of dream yoga centers on one basic psychological experience—that of "waking up" while in the dream state and recognizing that you are dreaming.

The waking part of it is precisely the same: While awake, you tell yourself that you are dreaming. Longchenpa writes:

> With unwavering attention hold (the idea) that (everything is) like a dream
> Regardless of whether you are walking, sitting, eating, moving about or conversing.
> When you are not separate from the idea that
> Whatever is present, whatever is being done, and whatever is thought about is all a dream,
> Then you train yourself in absolute non-subjectivity (by realizing that your dream)
> Has no truth-value, is but something flimsy, something ethereal, something evanescent,
> Something fleeting, something faint.[17]

This is one of the most easily sampled practices in the whole Tibetan bag of tricks, and it is also probably the easiest way possible to move deliberately into an altered state of consciousness. The practice is simply to tell yourself— right now, while you are awake—that you are really dreaming. Like any other meditation or mindfulness practice, this takes a certain amount of skill and/or determination to stay with it. Your consciousness will drift away from the practice just as it drifts away from an object of meditation, and will need to be guided gently back.

The dream-yoga practice is one that some people seem to find frightening, but if it is entered into in a certain spirit of playfulness, it becomes, as most people discover when they try it for a while, a pleasant experience. That spirit of playfulness is, in fact, a major part of what the dream yoga is about, as Tarthang Tulku explains:

> Dream yoga has been practiced for a long time. Why? Because the whole world has problems, and each individual has his or her own particular problems—something is uncomfortable, unbalanced or dissatisfying. . . . We have internal conflicts, an unhappy or unhealthy mind . . . maybe often, maybe all the time. "The main reason," say the dream philosophers, "is because you are so serious, because you *believe* in it and think *this* reality is true. You seriously believe your subjective viewpoint is real and unchangeable." So I take my reality seriously and find that it does not fit my desires and expectations. I have set up my ideas a certain way according to very specific, narrow rules. I have fixed ideas of happiness and so on. If reality does not fit, I struggle and suffer.
>
> Once you understand your experience as part of the dream, and that the dream is not a very solid or final reality, then you no longer have to treat your life as a serious problem. If you understand this completely, even painful experiences or mental conflicts become part of the dream. You may not have to suffer from your own interpretations. You become less tight and more flexible.[18]

The dream yoga is, like other vajrayana practices, a trick played on the trick. You play the game of pretending you are dreaming while another part of you knows you are really awake. But from the Buddhist perspective—remember that the word *buddha* means "awakened one"—the everyday, "going around in circles" mind is really in a dream world. The mind is experiencing its own *interpretation* of reality, its own *description* of the world, and calling that the real world. It cannot see itself in the act of interpreting or describing, and so thinks it simply perceives what is there.

And, although the dream yoga of course has no direct similarity to the various Western psychotherapeutic methods of dream analysis, some Westerners find when they begin to practice it that it is highly enjoyable to go all the way and interpret their waking experience according to their favorite system of psychology—discover a universe full of phallic symbols, Jungian archetypes, existential messages, or whatever. It is all part of discovering that you do interpret and describe the world to yourself; one way of understanding the nature of the game is to play it.

8. Rumors from the East

My first contact with Tibetan culture, so far as I can recall, came by the way of a comic-book hero called Phantasmo, Master of the Universe. Phantasmo was a formerly ordinary man who had gained supernormal powers, which of course he used in doing battle against the forces of evil. He had got his powers by going to Tibet, where he learned them from the lamas.

As I discovered later, Phantasmo was only one of a long line of characters out of popular fiction who had gone to Tibet and returned with remarkable superhuman abilities—ESP, teleportation, telekinesis, and the like. You may remember that the sinister Sax Rohmer creation, Dr. Fu Manchu, had learned certain secrets from the lamas. Then, in a somewhat different vein, there was James Hilton's novel *Lost Horizons*, about a fantastic land called Shangri-la, somewhere high in the Himalayas. All these fictional images reflected the ideas that people in the West had about Tibet, a land that only a handful of Westerners had ever seen. The travelers returned with strange tales of lamas, sorcerers, mystical practices. One concluded from the available evidence either that Tibet was a hopelessly benighted place, full of charlatans and primitive superstition, or, if you were more open-minded, that there really were such wonders left in the world. It was exciting to imagine that somewhere up among those high mountains there were holy men with magical powers, that (as was written in the Tibetan Book of the Dead) the lamas not only knew of states of consciousness experienced after death but had a technology for working with them. So for a half century or so, from the time the first European books about Tibetan civilization were published until the collapse of the Dalai Lama's government in 1959, Tibet served as the West's never-never land, the human imagination's last frontier of magic and mystery.

Even now, Westerners are often fascinated by Tibet's legendary character, and approach Tibetan Buddhism with the hope—or the fear, as the case may be—that it holds the key to the supernatural. I have seen people come to workshops and seminars at Tibetan Buddhist centers and press relentlessly after that subject: Can human beings really do that stuff? Is it possible to acquire superhuman powers? Can the mind remain conscious after death? The answer is, Yes, human beings can really do that stuff—but it isn't too important. It isn't exactly what Tibetan Buddhism is *about*. It is more important to relax, take care of your true needs, to understand the basic principles of Buddhism and open up to the nature of your own experience. The quest for the supernatural is a distraction, a dangerous ego trip.

Those warnings should be taken seriously, but we cannot entirely overlook that side of the Tibetan tradition. There is rather too much of it to overlook, for one thing; material that we would call "supernatural" is so large a part of the Tibetan culture that it is hardly possible to separate Tibetan Buddhism from it entirely and be left with anything that has much meaning.

This relates to the question of how Tibetan Buddhism fits into our culture. I have said that I think Buddhism will have to be somewhat domesticated in order to become a force in the lives of many Americans. But that does not necessarily mean it can be entirely reconciled with our official belief system, fit neatly within the official scientific/secular version of reality. That belief system is quickly changing anyway, and I suspect it will change a good deal more as Eastern disciplines are more fully assimilated into our culture.

Clearly the belief system in which Tibetan Buddhism flourished was quite different from our own. And I do not simply mean that the Tibetan people had different beliefs; I mean that they also had a different attitude toward belief itself. We like things to be either true or untrue. "True" things are experienced in more or less the same way by other people and are thus "verified" for us; the large category of "untrue things" includes that which is merely "symbolic," that which stands for something but is not literally true, and all the products of our own imagination—dreams and visions and so forth—which are "mental" and have no existence in the "real world." The Tibetan Buddhist belief system does not seem to work that way. If something can be imagined at all, it is accorded a certain reality; things can be symbolically true and literally true at the same time; products of the imagination such as the deities summoned up by vajrayana meditators are mental images, yet they are real. As for the other people and the social beliefs that give support to your perceptions of the world—they are in themselves events in your own field of consciousness, real but in a way illusory. When the distinction is made between an exoteric and an esoteric teaching, it is not a distinction between untruth and truth, but between levels of truth; it has to do with where you stand.

The Indian yogic lore that was incorporated into Tibetan Buddhism is full of accounts of *siddhis*, "powers," that can be mastered by the devoted practitioner. The Indian yogic sage Patanjali said it is possible, among other things, to see into the past and the future; understand all languages, including the sounds of animals; remember past lives; know the minds of others; become invisible; predict the exact time of your own death; obtain superhuman strength and sense perceptions; observe the distant workings of the universe; eliminate hunger and thirst; see divine beings; psychically enter the body of another person; walk on water; die at will; surround yourself in light; fly through the air; and become as small as an atom. He also warned the yogi against being caught up in self-importance by any of these powers; whatever power one has should be given up so that one may move beyond it, toward complete liberation.[1]

The accounts of Tibetan masters mention all the usual yogic siddhis, plus some that seem to have been especially important in Tibet. Among these are the *lung-gom,* or "trance walk," and the *tumo,* or "mystic heat."

Alexandra David-Neel, in her memoirs of travel in Tibet, told of her first encounter with one of the fabled lung-gom-pa lamas. She was traveling across a high table-land when she saw in her field glasses a black spot that appeared to be a man, but moving at an extraordinary rate of speed. One of her servants told her that the approaching figure was a lung-gom-pa and warned her not to talk to him, since it might be fatal to the lama if his trance were broken. She doubted the servant's superstitious belief that the lama was temporarily occupied by a god whose sudden departure would be fatal, but she refrained from stopping the lama as he passed:

> I could clearly see his perfectly calm impassive face and wide-open eyes with their gaze fixed on some distant object situated somewhere high up in space. The man did not run. He seemed to lift himself from the ground, proceeding by leaps. It looked as if he had been endowed with the elasticity

of a ball and rebounded each time his feet touched the ground. His steps had the regularity of a pendulum. He wore the usual monastic robe and toga, both rather ragged. His left hand gripped a fold of the toga and was half hidden under the cloth. The right hand held a *phurba* (magic dagger). His right arm moved slightly at each step as if leaning on a stick, just as though the *phurba*, whose pointed extremity was far above the ground, had touched it and were actually a support.

My servants dismounted and bowed their heads to the ground as the lama passed before us, but he went his way apparently unaware of our presence.[2]

Madame David-Neel later met other practitioners of the trance walk, and although she was never given the formal initiation and training in its method, she was told that it takes many years of training under an experienced teacher, during which the student learns a certain breathing technique and a mantra that is used for going into the correct state of deep meditation. Early evening is said to be a good time for performing the trance walk—especially when the traveler is fatigued but wishes to cover more ground—and it is considered advisable in maintaining the trance state to keep one's vision fixed on a particular star.

Lama Govinda, in his own account of travels in Tibet, told of a time he experienced the trance walk, when he was trying to make it back to his camp to escape spending a freezing night outdoors without blankets:

It was no longer possible to pick my way between the boulders that covered the ground for uncounted miles ahead of me; night had completely overtaken me; and yet to my amazement I jumped from boulder to boulder without ever slipping or missing a foothold, in spite of wearing only a pair of flimsy sandals on my bare feet. And then I realized that a strange force had taken over, a consciousness that was no more guided by my eyes or my brain. My limbs moved as in a trance, with an uncanny knowledge of their own, though their movement seemed almost mechanical. I noticed things only like in a dream, somewhat detached. Even my own body had become distant, quasi-detached from my will-power. I was like an arrow that unfailingly pursued its course by the force of its initial impetus, and the only thing I knew was that on no condition must I break the spell that had seized me.

It was only later that I realized what had happened: that unwittingly and under the stress of circumstances and acute danger I had become a lung-gom-pa, a trance walker, who, oblivious of all obstacles and fatigue, moves on towards his contemplated aim, hardly touching the ground, which might give a distant observer the impression that the lung-gom-pa was borne by the air (*lung*), merely skimming the surface of the earth.[3]

Lama Govinda did not think he had suddenly become a master of the lung-gom, but only that he had briefly discovered, in a moment of emergency, a natural human ability that the lung-gom training is designed to bring under the control of anybody who is willing to spend the required nine years of study and practice in order to master. He later visited one of the lung-gom training centers, a monastery in the upper Nyang Valley, where he had the opportunity to learn more about the practice. He became convinced that the trance walk was not meant to be an achievement in personal power but was rather an exercise in spiritual body/mind discipline, and that the word *lung* did not refer to the trance walker's apparent ability to fly through the air but to the breath control involved in the training process. (*Lung* means not only "breath" but also "wind" or "air," which in the Tantric medical system is regarded as one of the essential elements in the body, involved in many physical functions besides breathing.)

The heat-generating practice of tumo has also been reported by many travelers to Tibet. Like the lung-gom, it has obvious practicality, apart from its spiritual significance, in a land of great spaces and low temperatures. It builds upon the same attitudes and practices that are fundamental to all vajrayana pursuits: the devotion to enlightenment as the ultimate goal, superior to any personal accomplishments; the sense of "Tantric pride" or "cosmic confidence" in the unlimited capacities of nature; and long training in meditation, visualization, and breath control. The goal of the tumo practice is to learn how to generate heat from within one's own body, without the aid of any external devices.

Madame David-Neel witnessed the "final examination" used for testing the level of accomplishment of tumo students:

> Upon a frosty winter night, those who think themselves capable of victoriously enduring the test are led to the shore of a river or a lake. If all the streams are frozen in the region, a hole is made in the ice. A moonlight night, with a hard wind blowing, is chosen. Such nights are not rare in Tibet during the winter months.
>
> The neophytes sit on the ground, cross-legged and naked. Sheets are dipped in the icy water, each man wraps himself in one of them and must dry it on his body. As soon as the sheet has become dry, it is again dipped in the water and placed on the novice's body to be dried as before. The operation goes on in that way until daybreak. Then he who has dried the largest number of sheets is acknowledged the winner of the competition.
>
> It is said that some dry as many as forty sheets in one night. One should perhaps make large allowances for exaggeration, or perhaps for the *size* of the sheets which may in some cases have become so small as to be almost symbolical. Yet I have seen some respas dry a number of pieces of cloth the size of a large shawl.[4]

Whereas the lung-gom is a rare and semilegendary practice mastered by relatively few lamas, the tumo is more common; it is included in the "six yogas"—the basic teachings of Naropa, one of the great figures in Tibetan Buddhist history—and is mentioned frequently in Tibetan scriptures. The Tibetan poet-saint Milarepa wrote of spending the winter alone in a cave near Mount Everest, where he survived by practicing the inner-heat meditation:

The snow, as it fell on me, melted into a stream,
The roaring blast was broken against the thin cotton robe which
    enclosed fiery warmth,
The life and death struggle of the fighter could there be seen
And I, having won the victory, left a landmark for the hermits
Demonstrating the great virtue of *tumo*.[5]

Within the vajrayana tradition tumo is regarded as a secret practice, to be learned under the close guidance of a teacher and only after the appropriate preparatory training and initiation ceremonies. However, the details of the tumo meditation as handed down from Naropa are described in many places, and since this is now an open secret, we might examine it as an example of what an advanced vajrayana meditation technique is like, keeping in mind that it is not recommended for solitary experimenters.[6]

The tumo meditation is frequently practiced in conjunction with a physical exercise. In one exercise the practitioner breathes deeply, expands the stomach, and rotates the lower abdomen while sitting in a cross-legged position. The meditation should be performed in the early morning before any food or drink is consumed, and the serious would-be tumo practitioner is also cautioned against wearing warm clothing and building campfires to heat the body by external energy. The instructions also presuppose some familiarity with the three major *nadhis*, or "nerve channels," of yogic physiology—right, left, and center—which run from the base of the spine to the brain, connecting the chakras.

The meditator begins by concentrating on the navel-center chakra, and visualizes there a golden lotus out of which vibrates the mantric syllable *ram*. When the *ram* is clearly felt, vibrating like the sun in the golden center, there is then heard a second syllable, *ma*, vibrating just above it. Out of the *ma* emerges a feminine deity of a fiery red color, who is surrounded by flames. The meditator must then "become" this deity, concentrate on her until the identities of the meditator and the mentally created image have merged. Then still another syllable, *a*, is placed in the navel center; it vibrates with the color of fire and by intense concentration the visualized flame is then made to rise through the central channel directly toward the crown chakra located at the top of the head. Concentration should be focused primarily on the source of the flame, and, according to most texts, its ascent should proceed slowly and with caution toward the higher centers; some say it should not be permitted to rise above the throat.

When the visualized flame is permitted to rise, the central channel is also gradually allowed to expand. Originally as fine as a hair, it swells to the width of a finger, then that of an arm, and finally becomes as wide as the whole body. At this stage of the meditation, its highest level, the entire body is experienced as if on fire. The meditator may then gradually lessen its intensity by narrowing the central channel and returning the flame to its source.

The more hardheaded reader who might like some Western-style evidence of the effectiveness of the tumo practice is, at this point, pretty much out of luck. I know of no researcher who has been able to get a tumo master into the laboratory for tests of the sort that would meet Western scientific standards. However, we do have plenty of evidence that people can learn to modify their own bodily temperatures, and that advanced yoga practitioners can produce spectacular—and measurable—temperature changes. Elmer and Alyce Green, at the Menninger Foundation, have demonstrated that most people can learn rather quickly with the help of biofeedback training to increase the temperature of specific parts of the body, and one Indian yogi, Swami Rama, demonstrated in the laboratory that he could create a ten-degree temperature change in his hand in ten minutes.[7]

We are in about the same place with respect to the trance walk; that is, we have plenty of evidence to indicate that something *resembling* it is possible. The idea is not as foreign to us as it once was: A new generation of spiritual joggers are learning to use mantras and visualizations while running.[8] Writers such as Michael Murphy and George Leonard are now telling us that trance states and peak experiences are commonly attained by athletes and that we have all been so preoccupied with the competitive side of sports, so busy watching the scoreboard, that we have neglected the richest part of it—its *inner* nature, its value as a heightened state of psychophysical experience.[9]

But in this area East is still East and West is still West; the twain have not yet met, although they are no longer quite as far apart as they once were. Such phenomena as the trance walk and the mystic heat are still not reconciled with the prevailing Western ideas of what human and body can do, but they are no longer so totally remote from our thinking as they once were. The same is true of that remarkable piece of literature known as the Tibetan Book of the Dead.

The Book of the Dead came to the West in 1927; it was translated into English by a Tibetan lama, Kazi Dawa-Samdup, under the editorial supervision of a British anthropologist, W. Y. Evans-Wentz. Later it was published in a new edition with a preface by Carl Jung, who had found it to be a profound expression of Oriental psychology.[10]

The Book of the Dead is such a bizarre and fascinating work that it has been interpreted in several different ways by Westerners and has been the center of many variations on the exoteric-esoteric theme. We will look into some of those, but first it might be interesting to consider the context in which the book was used in Tibet, how it related to Tibetan customs and beliefs concerning death.

The most striking difference between Tibetan and American ways of dealing with death is the amount of attention given the corpse. In the United States we have surpassed most other civilizations in the amount of care lavished upon the dead body. We fill it with preservative chemicals, dress it in expensive clothes, beautify it with cosmetics, and then seal it away in caskets; we try to isolate it from the biological processes of the world, prevent it from decaying into the soil or becoming carrion for some hungry animal.

The Tibetans keep the body of the deceased around the house for a while, until the appropriate rituals are performed, and then carry it to a designated area where it is simply dumped onto the ground, left there to serve as food for the vultures and scavenging animals. Usually the man whose job it is to bring corpses to their final resting place will thoughtfully cut off a few pieces of meat and distribute them to whatever animals may be nearby at the time. (These places have for centuries been considered particularly good for meditation. Young monks are often directed to spend the night there sitting among the bones and putrefying corpses, musing on the transience of life.)

Normally Tibetan rituals for the dead are performed by one or more lamas from a nearby monastery. A lama specializing in astrology is called in to determine the precise time of death, which is ordinarily not the time of the observable physical death of the body but a time prior to that, usually several months earlier, when the life force was spent; this information determines the form of the rituals.

The Book of the Dead, whose Tibetan title means "liberation by hearing on the after-death plane," is read aloud daily in the house of the deceased. It is a set of instructions to the deceased about how to deal with the experiences encountered immediately after death in the *bardos*, or planes of existence, beyond ordinary life. It is addressed to a certain aspect of the psyche of the deceased, variously translated as the "knower" or the "consciousness principle." All this is done with the belief that the consciousness of the dead person is in some sense present and able to hear the instructions.

According to the Book of the Dead the afterlife experiences are a series of ordeals and opportunities for enlightenment; enlightenment in this case means the classical Buddhist concept of liberation from the cycle of death and rebirth. If all of the opportunities are missed, the consciousness will be reborn into another human body, usually after a period of forty-nine days.

The first opportunity, which presents itself at approximately the time of physical death, is called the "fundamental (or "primary") clear light." The deceased is told that this is a glimpse of the deepest and purest essence of the psyche, which is also the Buddha nature:

> Thine own consciousness, not formed into anything, in reality void, and the intellect, shining and blissful—these two—are inseparable. The union of them is the Dharma-Kaya state of Perfect Enlightenment.
>
> Thine own consciousness, shining, void, and inseparable from the Great Body of Radiance, hath no birth, nor death, and is the Immutable Light. . . ."[11]

If the deceased recognizes this light as the source of his or her own consciousness and identifies with it, liberation is achieved. Most people are unable to do this, for various reasons—fear, lack of understanding, lack of proper training while alive—and are condemned to further wandering in confusion on the after-death plane.

Only a few minutes after experiencing the primary clear light, the deceased has another, somewhat similar experience, called the "dawning of the secondary clear light." This time its force is less intense. Lama Dawa-Samdup, the book's translator, explains: "A ball set bounding reaches its greatest height at the first bound; the second bound is lower, and each succeeding bound is still lower until the ball comes to rest. Similarly is it with the consciousness principle at the death of a human body."[12]

If the consciousness fails to recognize the secondary light, it then progresses into the next stage, called the *chonyid bardo*.

One of the things that commonly happens in the first minutes after death (the book is not always too precise about time) is that the consciousness becomes aware of what is going on around the body. It sees the room and the people in it, hears the wailing of the mourners. This can be a time of great distress and confusion, since the deceased may not know that he or she is really dead and will try to talk to the living. Soon awesome and frightening sounds and lights are experienced, and some time after that the deceased begins to encounter apparitions.

The first set of apparitions to appear are peaceful deities, all of them, as described in the Book of the Dead, familiar figures from vajrayana symbolism. Each appears as a vivid reality, accompanied by a burst of bright color, and the deceased is advised to remember that these, too, are all merely manifestations of his or her own consciousness. Evans-Wentz speculates that for people of other religious faiths the archetypal mental forces that surface at this point might appear in different forms; the Tibetan sees the images known from tankhas and mandalas, but the Christian might encounter the Holy Trinity, the Virgin Mary, and the saints. They emanate from the psyche, like dreams; again and again the lama, reading from the Book of the Dead, reminds the deceased of this:

> O nobly-born, these realms are not come from somewhere outside (thyself). . . . They issue from within thee, and shine upon thee. The deities, too, are not come from somewhere else: they exist from eternity within the faculties of thine own intellect. Know them to be of that nature.[13]

The peaceful deities, like the clear lights, are opportunities for liberation; if the consciousness can recognize them as its own creations and thus become one with them, it has transcended the subject-object dichotomy that keeps it in its state of fearful confusion.

If you accept any of this as true, then the vajrayana disciplines we have discussed in previous chapters take on a whole new meaning: The meditations and the dream yoga are not only explorations of life but also preparations for death. The vajrayana adept has spent years learning how to summon up images from the deepest levels of the unconscious, recognize them as his or her own creations, and merge with them. The practice of dream yoga has provided a wealth of experience in "waking up" to the illusory nature of situations.

If he deceased fails to recognize the peaceful deities that appear during this seven-day period, he or she then proceeds to another yet more frightening stage wherein a series of wrathful deities appear. The peaceful and knowledge-bearing deities of the prior stage might have been enough to frighten most people, but the apparitions that now emerge are truly hideous: They come forth amid loud and terrifying sounds, are monstrous in form, waving weapons and drinking blood out of human skulls. One after another they appear, the most horrible beings the mind can imagine. The deceased naturally wants to run from them, but is told that these, too, are illusions—that they are in fact only different manifestations of the same beings that had been encountered earlier. (The idea that one's mental projections can have both a peaceful and a wrathful side is basic to vajrayana psychology.) As before, the deceased is advised to "own" the deities in order to achieve enlightenment and freedom.

If the deceased has not been able to heed the instructions, the consciousness principle then passes into the *sidpa bardo*, which may last as long as twenty-two days. New visions and ordeals will be experienced, and throughout all of them the consciousness is drifting toward the undesirable end of rebirth into another life.

Some of the experiences in the sidpa bardo resemble descriptions of heaven and hell and limbo in Christian writings. Persons with much evil karma will be punished—pursued by flesh-eating demons, beasts of prey, and angry crowds of people; there will be fierce storms, crumbling mountains, overflowing seas and roaring fires. Persons who have accumulated merit in their lives will have feelings of happiness and great ease, and those whose lives have been neither good nor evil will experience stupid indifference. Whatever the nature of the experience, the deceased is advised not to become attached to it; a state of meditation is best, but if the deceased does not know how to meditate, he or she should at least try to be mindful, to pay attention and analyze what is going on.

The Book of the Dead describes several adventures that may be experienced during this stage; the specifics are said to vary according to the different karmic influences of past experience and individual psychology. Toward the end of it, as the time of rebirth comes closer, the consciousness begins to see sexual images, fantasies of copulating couples. Even at this late stage, liberation is still possible and a variety of specific meditative techniques are suggested; the deceased is also given advice on how to choose a good rebirth if return to another life cycle cannot be avoided. The consciousness has some premonitory abilities at this point, and can vaguely foretell what kind of life it might be about to enter. In a strikingly Freudian passage, the book says:

> If (about) to be born as a male, the feeling of itself being a male dawneth upon the Knower, and a feeling of intense hatred towards the father and of jealousy and attraction towards the mother is begotten. If (about) to be born as a female, the feeling of itself being a female dawneth upon the Knower,

and a feeling of intense hatred towards the mother and of intense attraction and fondness towards the father is begotten.[14]

If the consciousness can let go of these feelings of attachment, there is still the chance that it will escape being reborn.

The Book of the Dead is a fascinating document, capable of being read at many different levels and/or put into a number of different pigeonholes: You could call it occult lore, a high religious scripture, or a primitive chart of the psychology of the unconscious. You can take it literally/exoterically, as a system for helping the confused shards of a dead person's consciousness to ascend to a higher level of being, or you can take it metaphorically/esoterically, as a symbolic representation of things that happen to living people.

In any case it is a thoroughly faithful expression of the essential ideas of vajrayana Buddhism. The advice read to the spirit of the deceased resonates with all the basic teachings: Pay attention; wake up; understand that your psyche participates actively in the creation of what seems to you to be external reality; let go of your fears and attachments. It says that if you can turn around and look directly at your mind, catch it in the act of spinning out its images and realize at the same time that it and the images are yourself, you are freed thereby from the delusions of ego.

The phenomena described in the Book of the Dead are also *physically* possible according to the yogic and Tantric concepts that underlie Tibetan Buddhism. If you equate the brain with the psyche—a perfectly respectable although much-disputed Western belief—then you naturally have a problem about *where* this knower is located in time and space and where it gets the energy to create such misery for itself if the body that supports it is now being digested by some Himalayan vulture. But in the vajrayana system there is considered to be a subtler body that corresponds to the physical body but is not in itself precisely physical. The *nadhis*, chakras, and other machinery of yogic practice are parts of this body and continue to function after the physical body is dead. In fact the Book of the Dead specifically identifies the chakras that are operating during the different bardo experiences; the peaceful and knowledge-giving deities are said to be projections of the heart and throat chakras, while the wrathful deities are creations of the head chakra, or brain. The book even identifies the regions of the brain from which the different wrathful deities emerge.

CARL JUNG wrote his commentaries on the Book of the Dead in the late 1930s, when it was being prepared for its first publication in German. He dealt with it as psychological material, but at the same time he understood clearly that it was the product of a culture in which psychology is not separated from metaphysics—in which a metaphysical plane of being and a state of consciousness could be regarded as more or less identical. "The background of this unusual book," he wrote, "is not the niggardly European 'either-or,' but a magnificently affirmative 'both-and.' " Jung compared the bardo planes to a map of the unconscious and the bardo experience to a form of therapy, a "penetration into the ground-layers of consciousness" similar to that undertaken in psychoanalysis.[15] But—here Jung resurrected his ancient quarrel with Freud—psychoanalysis was relatively shallow; it only penetrated to the depth of the *sidpa bardo* with its infantile sexual fantasies. Jung thought the psychological meaning of the Book of the Dead might become clearer to Westerners if they read it backward, passing through the Freudian imagery of the sidpa bardo to deeper levels where the archetypal forms of the collective unconscious appear as wrathful and peaceful deities. And although Jung did not explicitly say so in his commentary, his suggestion about reading backward through the bardos implies that at the deepest level of the unconscious would be found the utterly pure and formless vibration identified in the Book of the Dead as the clear light, which is entirely compatible with Buddhist psychology. The Jungian interpretation suggests that the interaction between the consciousness of the deceased and the attending lama is a last-chance psychotherapy—a massive cud-chewing of the contents of the unconscious with liberation into something inconceivably beyond human existence as the ultimate "breakthrough" to be achieved if the material is successfully processed.

In the 1950s Lama Govinda wrote still another introduction to the Book of the Dead, in which he pointed out that it could also be understood as equally—or even primarily—an esoteric document meant for the initiation of the living: "It is one of the oldest and most universal practices for the initiate to go through the experience of death before he can be spiritually reborn. . . . It is recognized by all who are acquainted with Buddhist philosophy that birth and death are not phenomena which happen only once in any given human life; they occur uninterruptedly. . . . The *Bardo Thodol* is addressed not only to those who see the end of their life approaching, or who are very near death, but to those who still have years of incarnate life before them."[16]

Lama Govinda thus offered a broader application of the Book of the Dead, and also a hint as to its source: It could be used as an initiatory guide to states of deep meditation, and it was probably written by people who had mastered the secrets of psychic exploration: "There are those who, in virtue of concentration and other yogic practices, are able to bring the subconscious into the realm of discriminative consciousness and, thereby, to draw upon the unrestricted treasury of subconscious memory. . . ."[17]

About ten years after Lama Govinda's commentary was written, at the height of America's infatuation with psychedelic drugs, Timothy Leary and two of his colleagues wrote an LSD travel guide based on the Book of the Dead. In it the authors reviewed the history of earlier Western attempts to understand the Book of the Dead. Jung, they concluded, had missed the boat; he had taken it all too literally: "Jung clearly sees the power and breadth of the Tibetan model but occasionally he fails to grasp its meaning and implication [which is] a detailed account of how to lose the ego; how to break out of personality into new realms of consciousness. . . . He comes close but never quite clinches it. . . . Jung settles for the exoteric and misses the esoteric."[18]

The authors, secure in the doper hubris of the 1960s, slid past the "both-and" part of Jung's commentary and concluded that the Book of the Dead was only an empty ritual except when taken, as Lama Govinda suggested, as a guide to psychic exploration. And this meant psychedelic exploration. The book's moment had finally arrived: "Now, for the first time, we possess the means of providing the enlightenment to any prepared volunteer."[19]

I don't mean to deny the applicability of the Book of the Dead to psychedelic experience; if it is a valid chart of the unconscious, then undoubtedly it can be of use in any states of being that give access to those levels of the psyche. Certainly the advice it gives to the deceased—not to panic or become "stuck," always to accept the images it encounters as parts of itself—are consonant with the best information on how to make the most of drug-induced states. But I also think we should give serious consideration to the possibility that the book is precisely what it says it is: a guide for the dead.

You may be familiar with the work of Raymond Moody, a young physician who has made a study of the experiences of people who "died"—people who had been resuscitated after being pronounced dead, or had come near death in an accident or illness, or had told others of their experience while dying. The material he has gathered is in some respects strikingly similar to the contents of the Book of the Dead. In a typical death experience

A man is dying and, as he reaches the point of greatest physical distress, he hears himself pronounced dead by his doctor. He begins to hear an uncomfortable noise, a loud ringing or buzzing, and at the same time feels himself moving very rapidly through a long dark tunnel. After this, he suddenly finds himself outside of his own physical body, but still in the immediate physical environment, and he sees his own body from a distance, as though he is a spectator. He watches the resuscitation attempts from this unusual vantage point and is in a state of emotional upheaval.

After a while, he collects himself and becomes more accustomed to his odd condition. He notices that he still has a "body," but one of a very different nature and with very different powers from the physical body he has left behind. Soon other things begin to happen. Others come to meet and to help him. He glimpses the spirits of relatives and friends who have already died, and a loving warm spirit of a kind he has never encountered before—a being of light—appears before him.[20]

Some of the accounts do not particularly resemble the Book of the Dead, but others, especially those dealing with the brilliant clear light and the confused attempts to communicate with the living, sound as though they could be right out of it. Dr. Moody wisely refrains from presenting his finds as "proof" of life after death. He asks only that anyone who disbelieves the accounts "poke around a bit for himself," which would not be a bad idea in regard to any of the subjects we have discussed in this chapter. Actually the accounts he has collected are not precisely accounts of death experiences; they are accounts of near-death experiences, or, to be even more precise, accounts of memories that still-living people have of things that happened to them (or that they say happened to them) while near death. That realm remains beyond our vision, and nothing we can say about it would conform to the Buddha's good advice in the Kalama Sutra: Believe that which you have tested for yourselves, and found reasonable.

Trance walkers, mystic heat, life after death. Strange things, indeed. As we look more closely at each of them and examine some Western parallels, the aura of magic thins a little but does not quite disappear. We are left with a sense of mystery, of something not yet fully understood. And the thing that is mysterious, if we think about it, is not the remote place called Tibet but rather human life.

9. More Tibetan Psychology: The Wheel of Life, the Higher Alertness, and the Ground of Being

Western psychology has produced many maps of the mind, attempts to chart the pathways of human experience. We have ways to measure and classify "character" or "personality structure," we have systems such as those of Freud and Jung that deal with the unconscious, and we also have a full storehouse of descriptions of mental deviation and illness. More recently other explorers—the humanistic and transpersonal psychologists—have taken off in new directions, studying self-actualization, peak experience, optimum health, and altered states of consciousness.

Tibetan Buddhism also has its own maps of consciousness, many of them, in fact. We have already looked at some: the concepts of samsara and nirvana, which are basic to all Buddhist thought; the dharma system, which is Buddhism's atomic table of thought processes; the symbolism and technology of vajrayana practice. In this chapter I would like to show you a few more.

Buddhist psychology does not have as many concepts of personality or character structure as Western psychology. Its emphasis on flux and change carries it away from such rigid surveys of the psyche. It tends to pay more attention to events, is more likely to describe human behavior in terms of situations rather than types.

I don't mean that Buddhism denies that people have persistent patterns of behavior, can easily get into a rut of creating for themselves similar situations throughout life. Buddhist writings sometimes compare every act to a scattering of seeds that take root and produce similar acts in the future. Yet, despite this, Buddhism always offers the possibility of breaking out of patterns; the enlightened person is free, which means that all of us are freer than we think.

ONE COMPLETE BUDDHIST SYSTEM of psychology is contained in a single picture: the "wheel of life." As commonly rendered by Tibetan artists, the picture shows a hideous demon holding a large circle divided into six wedge-shaped sections. The demon is Yama, the judge of the dead, and each section represents a different realm of life—the realm of gods, the realm of titans or demigods, the realm of human beings, the realm of animals, the realm of hungry ghosts, and the realm of hell beings. At the center or hub of the circle is a smaller circle containing a rooster, a pig, and a snake, chasing one another around and around. They symbolize the forces that keep people caught up in the samsaric round of existence: the rooster stands for greed, the pig for ignorance, and the snake for hatred.

You can read the wheel's symbols exoterically, as a diagram of six different kinds of existence into which one may be born in the endless round of reincarnation; the Book of the Dead deals with them that way, and some of its instructions have to do with striving to be born into one of the higher realms (gods, titans, human beings), and avoiding the lower ones (animals, hungry ghosts, hell beings). This exo-

The Tibetan Wheel of Life.

teric reading of the wheel's symbolism coincides with the more primitive beliefs regarding reincarnation—the idea that one may be reborn as a god or as some kind of lower animal—and also has some similarity to Christian doctrines regarding life after death.

You can also read the symbolism esoterically (on at least two different levels) as psychology. One way is to view each of the realms as a different type of human existence—a life script, to use the transactional-analysis term—lived out by certain kinds of people according to their karmic fortunes of personality type and socioeconomic status. At the top of the wheel is the realm of the gods, the people who have just naturally got it made. They are called *suras* or *devas*, and they are shown in a luxurious palace blissfully enjoying music, good company, and delicious food. The upper part of a fruit-bearing tree is shown in this section of the wheel, signifying that their riches are the karmic product of effort that has been performed by others. And although these people are fortunate they are still unenlightened; their chief sins are pride and complacency, born of a failure to understand that their condition is as temporary as everything else in human life. The Buddha appears in this realm carrying a lute, to remind them that their pleasures will all fade away, like the tone of the lute.

Next to the realm of the gods is that of the demigods, or *asuras*. This is an easily recognizable type: The power and money centers of the world—Washington, New York, Hollywood—are full of them. Their existence is one of continual striving, and their chief characteristic is envy. Their realm is one of the most fortunate, but the gods are better off than they are, and the asuras are obsessed by the knowledge that they are not quite at the top. The tree that bears fruit in the realm of the gods has its roots in their realm, and the asuras are usually shown trying to take the fruit by force. The Buddha appears to them holding a sword, which is commonly used by the Tibetans as the symbol of knowledge; they are urged to seek wisdom and peace of mind instead of power and wealth.

The last of the three higher realms is that of human beings. They have great freedom of choice, as is shown by the many different activities depicted in this section of the wheel—working, entertaining, giving birth. Some interpreters of the wheel symbolism say that one of the main features of this realm of life is bewilderment, because there are many different things to choose from, and most people, lacking a central purpose to their lives, wander aimlessly from one activity to another. This is the realm of ordinary human beings—not achievement-ridden demigods, but rather-well-off folks, something like America's middle classes, who have better lives than most people but still experience the sufferings of mortality. The Buddha appears to them carrying a begging bowl and a staff, suggesting the need to turn from their mundane existence toward a spiritual path.

Those are the three higher realms of the wheel of life. In the lower hemisphere are shown the realms of the animals, the hungry ghosts, and the hell beings.

The animals of the fourth realm are those people who go passively through the motions of life, following their instincts and urges, without the will or intelligence to take control of their own existence. They do not know the profound sufferings of the beings in the realms below them; they also do not know the freedom of ordinary human beings, the great aspirations of the demigods, or the bliss of the gods. This lethargy, this lack of awareness, is the recognizable characteristic of people in this category, and the Buddha shows them a book symbolizing the liberative power of clear thinking.

The hungry ghosts, or *pretas*, occupy the section just below the human beings. They are odd-looking creatures, and their physical shape is a vivid expression of the Buddhist view of greed and the problems it creates: Their bellies are huge but they have rather tiny throats, which makes it impossible for them to take in as much as they think they would like to have. Nothing seems to work out for them, and everything they try to do to get satisfaction only makes things worse. In some versions they are shown trying to drink water from a stream, but the stream turns to fire, which of course makes them even thirstier. The Buddha appears to them bearing a vessel of *amrit*, the elixir of the gods, to appease their misery. This can be read as a compassionate gift of the Buddha, but on another level it is meant to signify that these unfortunate beings need not only generosity from others but also the ability to cultivate generosity *toward* others as a way of rising above the self-centered craving that keeps them in misery.

The lowest realm of the wheel is a hellish, Dantean region whose occupants suffer all manner of physical pain. They are shown being tortured by demons, but the presence in this section of Yama, the god of the dead, holding up a mirror suggests that they are in fact being tortured by themselves. Hatred, the prevailing emotion of this realm, thus becomes self-hatred inspired by regrets of past wrong deeds and the knowledge of one's own inadequacies. (Buddhist psychology generally has this reflexive character, implying that whatever emotion you commonly feel from others is likely to be a way you commonly feel *toward* others—and toward yourself.) The hell region is usually shown with hot and cold areas representing the different ways that hatred, or self-hatred, can be experienced. Even here enlightenment is possible; the Buddha of this realm carries a flame of purification, signifying purification through suffering and also the esoteric concept that all negative emotions or drives can be transmuted into positive ones.

Looked at in this way, the wheel of life shows six basic types of people, the emotions that dominate their lives, and the specific methods considered by Buddhists to be best for obtaining liberation in each case. Perhaps in reading the descriptions you tried them on for yourself and found that one or another of the realms best symbolizes the way you feel about your life. Or perhaps you found the whole notion to be only a simplified rendering of Oriental morality with no particular application to your own life. In either case, let us go a step further, because there is yet another way to read the wheel's symbolism—a more flexible view that does not confine human existence to the rigidity of character types.

You can look at it as a description of *situations* or states of consciousness that everybody passes through again and again in the course of a day. Each of us has fleeting moments of being the self-satisfied god enjoying pleasure and forgetting the transience of it; the envious titan obsessed with the desire for success and tortured by the knowledge that other people are better off; the ordinary, rather confused human being dazzled by the load of responsibility and choice in the world; the lethargic and passive animal aware of nothing but instinctual drives; the frustrated ghost for whom nothing seems to work out right; the hell being tortured by the knowledge of inadequacies and past mistakes. The wheel keeps turning, and we slip from one realm to the next, hardly noticing that it happens.

Used in this way, the wheel's symbolism becomes a tool for mindfulness practice, a way of recognizing certain recurrent life situations, and also a way of dealing with them, since the Buddha figures that appear in each realm signify the specific kind of energy appropriate for working toward enlightenment in that particular situation. The wheel of life is one of the most common pieces of Tibetan visual symbolism. It appears in many different versions in most books on Tibetan art, and I am told that nearly every monastery in Tibet had its own mural of the wheel of life, usually painted somewhere near the entrance where it would be seen many times during the day by everyone who passed through the doors of the building. All of the ideas in it are found in Tibetan written scriptures, but its presence in visual form makes the message available to anyone who either cannot read or cannot spare the time for scriptural study. Also, as our current information on the workings of the two hemispheres of the brain tells us, symbolic information of this sort is processed by a different part of the brain from that which takes in the more linear/cognitive material.

The wheel of life is a kind of handy guide to the situations of everyday life, and it is also an expression of the

vajrayana idea that every life situation presents its own special opportunity for enlightenment. The quest is not confined to periods of meditation and religious activity; even
when you are being consumed by ambition or wallowing in
animal pleasures, the opportunity for liberation is there if
you can recognize the situation and understand how to use
it. This means, too, that no particular teaching is suitable for
all people at all times; the information or practice must be
appropriate to the occasion. This is one of the arguments for
working with a skilled teacher.

ALL OF THE REALMS depicted on the wheel are samsaric
states of attachment, but Buddhist psychology also has its
road maps of *higher* states achieved on the road toward full
enlightenment. Some Tantric schools identified four stages
of bliss, and Saraha in one of his stanzas curled a lip in the
direction of those mystics who were so foolhardy as to try to
describe in words the feeling of the highest state.

It may come as something of a relief to those who find
Buddhism a bit on the pessimistic side to learn that it does
have an extensive literature on the subject of peak experiences. The Tantric literature talks often of bliss, and although this is one of the elements that gives Tantrism its
reputation for hedonism, H. V. Guenther argues persua-
sively, with quotes from many Tantric sources, that the
Tantric ideal of bliss is really to be equated with the concept
of enlightenment: "The All-Buddha-Awareness which is experienced within ourselves," says one tantra, "is called Great
Bliss because it is the most excellent pleasure of all pleasures." Says another: "Enlightenment is bliss itself."[1]

I mention this not to revive the ancient argument about
whether the Tantrics are good guys or bad guys (I suspect
their ranks have contained plenty of both) but to get at the
essence of Tantric/Tibetan ideas about peak experience.
Since bliss is equated with enlightenment and enlightenment is held to be a natural human state, it follows that bliss

is present also. It is latent in the human consciousness, lost like a jewel in the mud. It can be rediscovered, but it is more or less invisible to the person whose thinking is too cluttered with concepts and anxious grasping. Bliss is not to be achieved by getting or doing something extraordinary; it is to be achieved by letting go, opening up, discovering what is there. It is like the clear sky, temporarily obscured by clouds, as in this passage from Longchenpa:

> Let your mind be where there is no frantic searching for
>   it by attention.
> At that time, by staying in the reach and range
> That is open and radiant, defying any propositions
>   about it, you are free from the distorting
>   subject-object division;
> There arises a sheer lucency that is like a translucent
>   and radiant phantom.
> There is no cessation of objects to be presented, but
>   there is no artificiality as to taking them as this
>   or that.
> There is pleasure naturally, shimmering, glimmering,
>   undisturbed.[2]

The kind of peak experience Longchenpa and the Tibetan Buddhists talk about is not the euphoric, "we just won the ballgame" sort of emotional state that many people think of in connection with such words as "joy" and "bliss." It is not *about* anything, and as a matter of fact there is a danger that when your feelings of happiness become connected to an object, take on the quality of euphoria, you are in fact slipping into a lower state of consciousness, climbing back on the samsaric merry-go-round. "Euphoric states ... remain the cause of fictitious being," says Longchenpa.[3]

Longchenpa presents an interesting diagram of four basic states of pleasant emotional content, showing how each of them has its "dark side" and how each interacts with the other.

In each case the feeling shown in capital letters is the

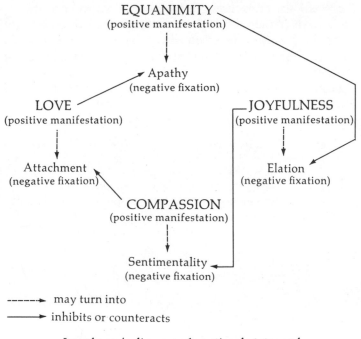

EQUANIMITY
(positive manifestation)

Apathy
(negative fixation)

LOVE
(positive manifestation)

JOYFULNESS
(positive manifestation)

Attachment
(negative fixation)

Elation
(negative fixation)

COMPASSION
(positive manifestation)

Sentimentality
(negative fixation)

------> may turn into
———> inhibits or counteracts

*Longchenpa's diagram of emotional states and
their negative counterparts.*

higher state, expressing the true and natural human being,
and the feeling shown just below is the condition you may
slip into if the experience becomes tinged with ego. One is
the manifestation of the true and free human intelligence,
and the other is the lie it can easily become—the caricature
of itself: Equanimity can lead to apathy, joyfulness to elation, compassion to sentimentality, love to attachment. But if
you understand this process, you can also retain your balance by using the appropriate emotion as an antidote: Love
counteracts apathy, compassion inhibits attachment, joyfulness dissolves sentimentality, equanimity brings you down
from elation. So if you are bored, let yourself love some-

body; if you become unhealthily attached to the one you love, extend your love beyond that individual to others who need it; if your compassion carries you into bleeding-heart sentimentalism, cheer up a little; if you cheer up too much, calm down.

All of this is rather good down-home advice, expressing the direct and practical side of Tibetan Buddhism. It is so clean and simple, in fact, that it is easy to lose sight of how closely it connects to one of the central principles of Buddhism, the denial of the reality of ego. Every one of these emotions, Longchenpa is saying, can be expressed out of the true essence of the human spirit or it can be expressed out of the false self-image called "ego." Each state has its own trap, and also its own escape hatch to authenticity and freedom.

THE NYINGMA CENTERS in America frequently organize their teachings on the subject of peak experience around the concept of *shin jong*, the "higher alertness" or "natural awareness." Shin jong compares to ordinary states of ego-centered attention as love compares to attachment. It is a free and open high-level state of consciousness in which is experienced both great relaxation and great energy.

Consider, before we talk more about shin jong, a state of its opposite—ego-centered attentiveness. One archetypal case that we are all familiar with is that of a student sitting in a classroom or library on a sunny day, studying but not wanting to. In such a situation the mind keeps wandering off into fantasies and fears, the attention keeps trying to affix itself to some object other than the book, and the student has to force his or her attention back to the subject of the text. The whole effort is entangled with self-concepts, memories, hopes of the future—"I want to become a doctor," "I've been punished in the past for not studying," "I'll just finish this chapter and then take a break." The body is building up tension; the emotional state is one of sluggishness or downright depression. You know what that feels like, of course;

but note how strongly present in such situations is the sub-ject-object dichotomy—the sense of the "I" with all its needs and agendas, and the sense of other things, some of which are desirable and some not. "Out there" is something that is making you uncomfortable, and "out there" also is some-thing that would make you happy.

Then consider Tarthang Tulku's description of a state of higher awareness:

> The experience of our own inner awareness is definitely not a *re*-experience. It is not a memory or a projection. It is not like "this" and not like "that." It is not associated with any "thing," but a perfect, beautiful, immediate and spontaneous presence. This natural awareness becomes its own experi-ence, but without a tight clinging to the past moment and without trying to project the next moment—without, we might say, any experience or any experiencer. It is totally free of fear, guilt, worry, expectations, projections, fixations, ideas, concepts, judgments, images or taking positions. When we experience or become involved with this open na-ture, nothing is lacking, for this "lacking" is simply the projection of our unawakened ignorance. There is nothing to defend and nothing to do, yet at the same time the natural movement of this awareness eliminates all obstacles to see-ing things just as they are, and the natural expression of this awareness provides the perspective which makes all positive action possible.[4]

Veteran readers of Buddhist writings may find the de-scription of the shin-jong state similar to many descriptions of nirvana or enlightenment, which is quite correct. Shin jong is a glimpse of nirvana, a space of time in which you sample a condition of pure awareness that can spread and deepen until it sweeps away the last traces of the delusion of ego. The state can come upon you spontaneously—every-body has had an experience of that pure, radiant awareness at some time or another—or it can be sought out, if you know how.

First of all, know the state; have a clear sense of what shin jong is about. There was a time, of course, when you did not need any such fancy ideas, but you are much more sophisticated now and you need a little more sophistication yet to get back to your own simplicity. Just don't be impressed by it; all you are doing is finding again the clean awareness of childhood, which is there as strong and fresh as ever beneath the obscurities. (Buddhist writings often compare the mind to a sky filled with clouds, or a mirror covered over by a layer of dust.)

Knowing the state means having some feel for the territory, an openness toward the possibility of it. This is a tricky business, because Western ways of knowing—precise definitions, rigid sets of expectations—may for some people block the way into a state of higher alertness, or guarantee slipping out of it immediately as soon as it begins to be experienced. But it can be known; there are guidelines, signposts. The Buddhists writings use such terms as "stillness," "openness," "clarity," "peace," "relaxation," "brightness," "joy," "spaciousness," "freedom," "freshness," "newness." Think of times when life has felt that way, and be willing to experience such a state again; but take care that the experience is not about anything in particular, fixed neither on an object that creates it ("I'm happy because . . .") nor on any concepts of yourself as experiencer. "Create a thought," says one Buddhist proverb, "but do not dwell anywhere."

Once you have some feel for it, going into the state is no big deal: You slow down, take it easy, pay attention, open up. Let the eyes relax, so that they feel comfortably open and are neither straining to look at anything in particular nor struggling to avoid anything. Let the rest of yourself be the same way. Relax the breath so that it becomes calm and seems to be coming and going of its own volition. You can try walking about a bit, very softly and slowly, feeling the subtle energy in your body and the easy shifting of your weight. If you are doing something, try doing it at half speed, slowing down and letting it become a gentler, more peaceful motion. As you tune in to what is happening, a sense of warmth and energy rises in the body, moving softly in the bloodstream, stirring in the stomach and heart and head. The only thing to do with the feeling is to let it come, until it becomes larger and fills all the space of your existence.

You can move into the shin-jong state at any time, but most Americans who work with the practice find they need a special time and place when they can let go of their roles and responsibilities. I have talked to quite a few people who have experienced states of high awareness while driving. The following is an account, by a businessman who had been exploring shin-jong practice, of a drive along a California freeway. Note that in this case the prevailing theme is one of newness, although it takes place on a familiar stretch of road only a few miles from his home:

> I was driving along the freeway and I said, "I'm going to try to experience all this as though it were happening for the first time. What is the state where I don't know how to drive, I don't know what a car is? What's it like where I simply don't have any labels, whatsoever?" And I simply started quieting down inside. I was holding the wheel, and I was looking, and suddenly what happened inside was as if there was somebody looking out from my eyes, and I was just there, without labels, looking. It was a kind of a shift— everything shifted, and all of a sudden everything was brand new. It was like I had never seen that country before in my life. There were no reference points, no comparisons. And the thing just opened up like an absolutely glorious vista. I said, "Wow, what is this all about?" And this went on until I got to the tunnel, so it must have been about a 12-to-15-minute drive. Then comparisons started creeping in, and the flavor was no longer the same.

The shin-jong state is a free-flowing appreciation of whatever presents itself to the consciousness, and is not in any sense problem-centered or concentrated thinking, yet the Buddhists value it highly for its productivity. Here is Tarthang Tulku on that subject:

> One may envision Shin Jong as a pleasant escape, divorced from the problems of the world. Such is not the case. Aside from a lighter and more joyful state of mind Shin Jong produces interesting side-effects for memory, imagination and communication. By loosening the tight hold of a particular subject (me) relating to a particular object (tree, job, baby), Shin Jong opens the gates of past eidetic memory. The multi-dimensional receptivity of Shin Jong encourages a playfully agile imagination. By refusing to objectify people with whom we deal into solid, static permanence, Shin Jong allows us to deal with others—as they are at this moment— on the same level with ourselves. Finally, the spacious receptivity of Shin Jong clarifies the muddled mind to such an extent that such psychic phenomena as clairvoyance and telepathy are known to occur.[5]

To understand the shin-jong state is also to prepare yourself to venture into one of the most difficult subjects in all of Tibetan Buddhist psychology: the "ground-state," or *kun-ji.*

SINCE KUN-JI is held to be fundamentally indescribable, it does not easily lend itself to being written about; but without taking a peek at the subject we miss something very important about Tibetan psychology. We never even glimpse the depth and subtlety of its analysis of the nature of thought.

You will recall our discussion of the dharmas, the basic atoms of mental process as analyzed by the early Buddhist schools of India. According to that system, human consciousness is a sequence of aggregations of particles of mental energy that come together in a certain pattern and disappear, to be replaced by another aggregation, each of these combinations taking place within an immeasurably small period of time. At one point I compared them to the pointillist paintings of Seurat, in which a number of dots combine to form a picture, a *Gestalt,* a whole instant of being alive and human that contains within it all our sense experiences and thoughts, including our memories and illusions of permanence.

If we go a bit further with that analogy, we can then compare kun-ji to the canvas on which the dots are painted. It is the ground-state below (or between) thoughts, the invisible foundation of whatever is going on in your psyche at any moment.

We can become aware of kun-ji, according to the Tibetan Buddhist teachers, although it cannot be apprehended by any of the senses. In a certain sense it would be more accurate to say that you are always aware of it; you just may not be aware that you are aware of it. Like many of the other subjects dealt with in Tibetan philosophy, it is present but subtly present, easy to overlook. The exact nature of the kun-ji varies; Tibetan psychology identifies several different ground-states, some of which are "lighter" in quality and others "heavier" or "denser." One American psychologist who has worked extensively with kun-ji states, Gay Luce, compares the heavier kun-ji to "a densely peaceful state, experienced briefly by athletes after a maximum exertion, a blankness experienced after deep breathing exercises or orgasm."[6] Dr. Luce speculates that the deep kun-ji state resembles drunkenness, and that alcoholism may be an unconscious urge to penetrate to deeper ground states that are sensed as comfortable or familiar.

Becoming aware of kun-ji is a more subtle or refined level of mindfulness practice; besides paying attention to what you may be thinking or feeling, you begin to pay attention to the underlying tone and observe that it often changes—something is there underneath or behind your thoughts and perceptions that has a different feel to it at different times. You may notice that after a period of meditation, something is different; you can't put your finger on it, but something very essential has changed. It is not quite the same as a shift of mood, which is a change of emotions and physical sensations—something finer than that, and in itself nothing.

The concept of kun-ji, the practice of developing a fine-tuned awareness of the airy and intangible levels of experience beneath our conscious thought and feelings, leads toward an understanding of your own experience that is more profound than a knowledge of states of consciousness such as those we have been discussing in the earlier part of this chapter—the situations depicted on the wheel of life, the emotional fine-tuning taught by Longchenpa, the peak experience of shin jong. It has to do with getting a glimpse of the root of emotions, the neutral ground out of which we create our experience of the world. To develop a sensitivity toward the ground of consciousness is to gain an enhanced understanding of the transience and insubstantiality of the thought forms that are created out of it; that understanding is best described as "enlightenment."

10. Enlightenment: Learning and Unlearning

We come back to enlightenment, a subject that has inspired and infuriated the followers of the Buddha for 2500 years. The concept of some other way of being in *this* life distinguishes Buddhism from all those beliefs whose chief preoccupation is salvation in the world to come.

Enlightenment is so close to the very center of all Buddhist thought that there is very little we can get out of Buddhism without it. A person raised in a society where Buddhism is the established religion would likely have no trouble accepting this concept, but it presents certain problems to a Westerner. If you do not consider yourself already enlightened, then you can't know what "enlightenment" is; the word merely stands for some state of being that is supposed to have been achieved by Lord Gautama a long time ago in India, and perhaps by other extraordinarily holy people. To accept it is to perform an act of faith, no different from deciding to accept the teachings of Christ or Muhammad. The Buddha's advice about accepting only what you know in your own experience becomes either a lie or a paradox: Why should you waste your time on a lot of practices to get yourself into some condition that you don't even know exists? And the vajrayana assertion that samsara and nirvana are the same thing, that the Buddha nature is the way you already are, is even more paradoxical: If you are already in nirvana and nirvana is bliss, how come you don't feel blissful? What validity can there be in the first noble truth if the natural state of human life is not suffering but peace and joy?

A Westerner who has dipped a toe into Buddhist waters might answer that these paradoxes are inherent in words and logic, that Buddhism is a nonintellectual system, neither literary nor logical. That is not entirely true: Buddhism has produced an immense amount of writing, and the study of logic is highly valued in most schools of Buddhism. The sages of Buddhism's classical era in India used to have debates that were major national events, the Super Bowls of their time. Debating and logic were also taught in the Tibetan monasteries. (The Tibetans, with their usual penchant for getting the body into the act, even developed mudras for debators—curious physical positions with much crouching and pointing of fingers.)

Words and logic do have their places in the Buddhist approach to learning; they are tools to be used with an understanding of their limitations. Words do not describe enlightenment or any other state of consciousness; they can only serve as hints or helpers along the way. They are guidelines to be used in a process of self-discovery and self-education. Words can bring you to a place where you can pay attention to such things as shin jong, experiences which are in themselves nonverbal. You go into those spaces and come out of them, perhaps, with words of your own that you use to describe your experience to others. But the map, as the general semanticists are fond of pointing out, is not the territory. Words that attempt to describe the silent and invisible foundation of your conscious experience, kun-ji, serve only to help you notice something that was there but that you did not previously think about. In the absence of such words—and the English language is strikingly deficient in words that describe the more subtle and transcendent states of consciousness—we develop socially conditioned *scotoma*, blind spots in the field of vision that make us incapable of contacting large parts of our own reality. We need some words, oddly enough, to give us courage to explore and appreciate the enormous wordless spaces of human existence.

The function of logic in Buddhist philosophy is not exactly to prove the correctness of its doctrines—nirvana, anatman, and so forth—but to demonstrate the fragility of the concepts that oppose them. So much of the work along the Buddhist path is unlearning. Prove that there is anything at all in the universe that is not a flow of subjective perceptions of it; prove that there is a "you" that exists separately from your environment; show where the boundary between you and your environment is located. In one of the classic works of Tibetan Buddhism, the eleventh-century text called the Jewel Ornament of Liberation, the author sets out to demolish the concept of the self by asking where the self resides— in the body, in the mind, or in a name? He then proceeds to show that the body is no more than a collection of the elements that compose it, that the mind is something that has never been seen (by ourselves or by anyone else), and that the name is merely a convention. Nothing with any permanence or fixed boundaries can be proved to exist.[1] The commonsense assumptions that support our ordinary world view cannot stand very much logic; they self-destruct. They can only live in a twilight of awareness, where we do not look at them too closely but only admire them because they are terribly respectable.

In Buddhism, *prajna*, "discriminative awareness," is valued as a tremendously important intellectual quality. It is the sword that so often appears in Tibetan symbolism, the weapon the Buddha offers to the asuras, the jealous gods, in the Wheel of Life. It is the analytical logic that cuts through mental clutter. (This particular kind of intellectual strength, by the way, is considered to be of primary importance only in earlier stages of growth. Later that hard-edged wisdom becomes less important, and another kind of wisdom, jnana—sometimes translated as "pure awareness"—develops. The Tibetan teacher Petrul Rinpoche compares this more mature wisdom to that of an old cow grazing happily in the meadow; there is total involvement and completion, with nothing lacking and nothing to be overcome.²)

WORDS ARE, at best, guidelines into subjective domains that are not in themselves verbal; logic in Buddhism is a kind of intellectual bulldozer that loosens some of the intellectual barriers to self-discovery.

But this doesn't prove—does it?—that there is any such state as enlightenment. The questions remain: Why bother with any of this? What is it about Buddhism that has attracted so many people for so many years? How have so many people been persuaded to pursue a goal they cannot see?

An appropriate vajrayana answer to this would be that you *can* see the goal, that everybody knows intuitively that there is a way of being more direct and true with life. "Not being enlightened" is just a game we play because we are afraid—we have been taught to be afraid—of letting go and opening up to the way we really are. So we pursue the goal because at some level we recognize that it exists, even though we may not be able to describe it in words. "my heart has followed all my days/something i cannot name," wrote the literate cockroach Archy in the Don Marquis stories, speaking for a lot of us.

That's one answer. Another would be that Buddhism doesn't really ask you to believe anything. Don't get hung up thinking about enlightenment. Just pay attention to your life; investigate it closely; be awake in your experience and really look at how you feel and what you are thinking. You can, if you want, accept the idea of enlightenment as an hypothesis, something unproved, to be tested out in your own experience—but you don't really have to do that. You can merely operate on the respectable assumption that it is better to pay attention to your life than to wander about in a stupor, that the unexamined life (as Socrates put it) is not worth living. This is an approach to Buddhism that has appealed to many rational-minded Westerners.

And there is a third answer, which I would like to explore now: Is enlightenment all that foreign to us after all? Aren't the experiences Buddhism deals with and the goal it envisions really familiar to all of us? I mean that we don't just sense the truth of it *intuitively*, but actually have many experiences in the course of our lives that give us a conscious and rational understanding of enlightenment.

I am not arguing that we understand what complete enlightenment is about, what it is like to be entirely free of delusive concepts or attachments—only that we do know something about the growth process of moving in that direction. We know what it feels like to become a little more enlightened than we used to be.

What the Tibetans mean by "enlightenment" is "growing up." They see it as a matter of discovering (you might also say "rediscovering") the essential and natural wholeness that is the human being's natural birthright. And this means it is part of everybody's experience.

True, most of us don't ever fully grow up—we die first—but throughout our lives we have many opportunities to experience for ourselves what growth feels like. We all go through periods when we are conscious of beginning to experience and comprehend the world in a new way, put the pieces together differently, and as we do so we may notice also that we not only *add* something but also *let go* of certain things; some things that seemed terribly important to us no longer have their power; some things that we used to believe no longer seem true; some things that were once great fears or obstacles no longer seem so threatening; some things that we once wanted we no longer want: "When I was a child," goes the Biblical passage, "I spoke as a child, I understood as a child: But when I became a man, I put away childish things."[3]

Psychological growth, putting away childish things— these are also central concerns of psychotherapy, and many Westerners have discovered by now that the Buddhist practice and Western psychotherapy are in some ways remarkably similar. Basically they are learning experiences, technologies of growth.

One of the things we know about human development is that you can't make somebody grow up. An adult can't simply explain to a child what it is like to be an adult and thereby have the child mature. The child just can't take in that information; he or she has to do the growing. Similarly, a therapist can't simply explain to a patient what it is like to be sane (read "well balanced," "mature," "fully functioning") and thus effect a successful therapy.

Herbert Fingarette, whose essay on this subject I mentioned in the preface, explains: "Strange to say, in the literature of psychoanalysis, it is difficult to find a sensitive and extensive account, in nontechnical language, of the 'feeling' of one's 'subjective' experience *after* successful analysis."[4] He interviewed a woman who had had successful therapy, and he found it was very hard for her to tell what had changed. She tried to tell how she felt about another woman with whom she formerly had strong conflicts. All she could say about it was, "I still may think that what she's doing is wrong at times, but it doesn't matter much. That is, well, I would defend myself if she did anything wrong to me . . . but, well, I wouldn't *dwell* on its being wrong. I'm just not involved. It doesn't matter *in the same way.*'[5]

Fingarette points out that when he attempts to get the woman to talk about how she has changed, she "finds herself forced to use locutions which she realizes are unusual, contradictory, inadequate, and in constant need of corrections which are in turn bound to be inadequate. It is clear that she is trying to put something into language which the language is not equipped to communicate in any routine, news-reporting fashion."[6] She does not, of course, fail entirely; we can understand at least part of what she is trying to tell us, especially if we can identify similar experiences of our own. But there is no guarantee that we will understand; there is certainly no guarantee that the woman could simply talk somebody else out of a similar neurotic conflict.

Fingarette came to the conclusion that everyday language is essentially a "language of self." What it does best is to communicate ego states, subject-object dichotomies, dualism, attachment. True, there are words to describe other states—there is compassion, for example, and selflessness—but these words are very easy to misunderstand. If you haven't experienced the state the words describe, you take them to mean whatever it is you *have* experienced.

This is a danger that is ever present if you try to understand Buddhism merely through reading without also undertaking some form of self-observation. Words can help, and they can also mislead: You can read about equanimity, but unless you have discovered and mastered the state of being energetically at peace, you will think equanimity is apathy. You may think these Buddhists are trying to tell you to vegetate and not give a damn about anything. Who wants to be that way? And so it goes.

The language is not *always* misunderstood. The history of psychotherapy is full of situations in which a patient suddenly gets the message; something falls into place, and life is changed. The annals of spiritual practice contain many similar anecdotes: Zen is replete with parables in which the master mutters a few words and the scales fall from the disciple's eyes. The real message of all these stories is that *when you are ready,* verbal communications can be of great value. The recipient of the message is an active participant in the communications process, and helps create the meaning it contains. At the proper stage of growth, certain information can be taken in and used. And when that happens, we look with wonderment at the information, which may be something we had heard a hundred times before, and say, My God, *that's* what that's about! That experience is one of the many times in life when we are living the enlightenment process.

The process of growth involves taking in new information, integrating it into our world view, and it also involves letting go of something: "When I became a man, I put away childish things." In the post-therapy interview quoted by Fingarette, the woman has a very hard time talking about how she feels *now,* although she knows she is much happier; she tends to point out the ways she *doesn't* feel, the destructive patterns she has let go of. Growth is not only opening up to something new but dropping attachments.

Attachment is certainly one of the fundamental elements of Buddhist thought, and it is another one of those concepts that can easily get filtered through the language of self and come out meaning something quite different from what Buddhism has in mind. We end up believing, as many people do, that the basic teaching of Buddhism is to give up everything.

But you find very little in the Tibetan teachings about whether "things," possessions, are "good" or "bad"; you find very little talk about the moral superiority of poverty or the simple life. True, people in Tibet lived much simpler lives, in terms of material possessions and comforts, than we do, and there were solitary holy men who got along with scarcely any material comforts at all, but most people, including most Buddhists, made themselves as comfortable as they could and did not pretend to be immune to ordinary

pleasures. What you find in the Tibetan teachings is an emphasis on the destructive nature of certain *states of mind,*
commonly described by such words as "grasping" and
"craving."

Americans commonly approach Buddhism with guilt
feelings about the level of their consumption of material
goods (a reasonably appropriate way for members of the
most wasteful civilization in human history to feel) and want
some guidance as to what they should do about it. They
don't get much. Buddhism offers the doctrine of the middle
way, which is sound advice, but that middle way is pretty
wide. Ask specific questions, and you get answers that don't
seem to fit together: Sure, there are wealthy people who are
enlightened. Sure, the pursuit of material goods is a hangup.
It all depends.

You will find it hard to understand the Tibetan Buddhist teaching on attachment by talking about the external
trappings of life—yours or anybody else's. To get it you
have to work from the ground up, starting with the basic
practice of watching and analyzing your own experience.
You watch the thoughts and sensations come and go, note
precisely which ones are pleasant, which ones are unpleasant, which ones are neutral. That is where your attachments
are to be discovered and overcome. Attachment is a process
of holding on to experience, categorizing it, turning it into
words, trying to make it be like something that happened in
the past or something you think it ought to be. "The world is
enslaved by thought," says Saraha.[7] The end to that enslave-
ment, say the Buddhist scriptures, is to *see* the true nature of
thoughts. As that is done, a great inner spontaneity develops. "A mind which has found peace . . . does not abide anywhere and is not attached to anything."[8] "Free from the
domination of words you will be able to establish yourselves
where there will be a turning about in the deepest seat of
consciousness. . . ."[9]

The growth process is a letting-go of the grasping, craving way of dealing with your own experience, your own thoughts. This does not mean that you reject any particular idea or feeling; the notion that certain thoughts are unthinkable is in itself an attachment. Any thought may pass through your mind; you do not have to act upon it in any particular way; nor do you have to become connected to it and think it is *you*. It is simply what it is. That is what the doctrine of nonself is about.

> For there is suffering, but none who suffers;
> Doing exists although there is no doer;
> Extinction is but no extinguished person;
> Although there is a path, there is no goer.[10]

The woman Fingarette interviewed about her therapy might have thought, before she went into it, that it would have the result of sweeping away her feelings of anger toward and disapproval of the other woman. But it didn't do that; it changed something in how she felt about the feelings.

Undoubtedly a change in the way you deal with your flow of thought processes will have repercussions in the way you deal with people and objects and events. Buddhism teaches that our feelings toward people and objects are in large part projections: Out of our craving we make certain things desirable; out of our fear and hatred we make certain people into villains. When the thoughts are clearly analyzed, the feeling of anger may arise, but it cannot affix itself in the same way: "For a person who has made the . . . . analysis, there is no hold for anger, any more than there is for a grain of mustard-seed on the point of an awl, or for a painting in the sky."[11] That is the poetic rendering of a Buddhist scripture. The woman in Fingarette's study merely says, "It doesn't matter in the same way."

As anger fails to attach itself in the same way to people, as craving fails to attach itself in the same way to things, our dealings with the external world do change. We may very well find that some of our needs for material things drop away, and begin to live more simply. But this is not a matter of having adopted some code of moral behavior, Buddhist or any other; it is a natural expression of an improved understanding of our real needs. Nothing is being sacrificed at all, so there is no reason to get puffed up about one's moral superiority. "Renunciation," says a Zen master, "is not giving up the things of this world, it is accepting that they go away."[12]

Not only material needs but also many beliefs and anxieties drop away naturally, according to the Buddhist writings on spiritual growth. Gampopa, author of the Jewel Ornament of Liberation, says that at a certain level of development, when you catch a mere glimpse of the truth, an outer layer of primitive beliefs about reality "is stripped like bark from a tree" and you spontaneously become free of five types of fear, which he identifies as: (1) fear of not making a living, (2) fear of having a bad reputation, (3) fear of death, (4) fear of being reborn into evil lives, and (5) anxiety about passing through unpleasant situations in your own lifetime.[13] Such changes are described as natural payoffs of strict self-analysis.

However mysterious and inscrutable some aspects of Buddhism may appear, there is absolutely no secret about its most important teaching. The information is available everywhere, and the path is wide open. The instruction is, simply, "Pay attention. Observe your thoughts and feelings. Look closely at what is going on. Tell yourself the truth."

WE ALL have experiences of feeling an attachment drop away. It is so ordinary we don't even talk about it much. But we know; becoming more mature means becoming less attached to a lot of things—old beliefs, compulsions, fears, needs.

We know, but we also happen to be living in the middle of a society that is an organized conspiracy against that knowledge. We are continually barraged by information that tells us to *become attached.* Our environment is saturated with such messages. You can scarcely hear a single song without being informed that the way to become happy is to find precisely the "right" person, hang on to him or her as tightly as possible, and believe that without that person all life is a joyless desert. Our love songs and love stories are written in the language of self; they talk of love, but they teach attachment. They teach us to create in our minds an image of happiness, to go through life searching for people and situations that will fit that image, to cling hungrily to whatever resembles it and to reject—sometimes bitterly— whatever does not. The divorce courts are full of people who have come to the conclusion that the other person was not doing what we are all taught that another person is supposed to do—i.e., make life happy.

Meanwhile, other instructions on how to be attached are continually being hurled at us from all directions. The advertising media do their best to get us hooked on things— "happiness is a new car"—while the government and the educational institutions bind us to our country—"my country, right or wrong"—and our peer groups render us help-lessly dependent on concepts of who we are, how we should act, and what we must believe in. All of these influences conspire to create in each of us patterns of thought that have certain similarities, although they vary greatly in their de-tails: (1) a fictitious, rigid, and socially conditioned self-image, and (2) a fantasy world filled with objects and people that we think will make our lives meaningful if they can be obtained in the proper quantities.

So, even while you may follow the practice that is guaranteed to cut through attachments, you will not find it easy, because the social environment is working in precisely the opposite direction.

This is why the process called "spiritual growth," or "progress toward enlightenment," is even harder than progressing from childhood through youth into adulthood. In that earlier kind of growth you could learn from everybody around you, take in the society's messages, model yourself on the people you knew and the images of people you encountered in books and movies and television. But now you find that you have created a false self and there is another you yet to be discovered; you have to unlearn everything, question every assumption, and look for yourself at every aspect of your life. Society can't help you much, because society is largely a structure of egos, hustling one another around in samsaric circles and chattering in the language of self.

This is true, to some extent, of all modern societies. Other nations may not share our craving for underarm deodorants and pocket calculators, but they all have their own organized delusions that militate against personal growth outside of approved channels. In almost any society the person who has much luck becoming free of attachments stands the risk of being regarded as a fairly odd citizen. Almost any social milieu has its ways of reinforcing your hangups.

Hence the Buddhist tradition of the *sangha*, the congregation of seekers who support one another along the path. The Buddhist sangha, civilization's oldest established floating reference group, serves the purpose of making the search a little less lonely. This is also, of course, one of the functions of a teacher, who at certain stages of one's development may become the ultimate authority figure, whose advice becomes more compelling than all other social pressures.

The teacher—what Americans usually call a "guru," what Chögyam Trungpa prefers to describe as a "dangerous friend"—helps in both the learning and the unlearning parts of the growth process. Remember that in the Buddhist psychology of self-development you are not permitted the luxury of holding on to any fixed concept of the self. You must, as you grow, repeatedly discard your old ideas of what growth is, what you are, what you are to become. This is a hard thing to do alone.

The mind continually tries to build upon change, to turn experiences into belief systems. Buddhism relentlessly breaks up all such developmental logjams; it says that whenever you become content with what you are doing, whenever your beliefs rigidify, you are in trouble. Even that most sublime and ineffable of Buddhist concepts, shunyata, is not allowed to become sacred. Gampopa, while discussing the great merits of the shunyata experience, also cites several texts warning of the dangers of the shunyata *ideology.* "Those who believe in Shunyata," declares one text, "are said to be incurably ill."[14] Tibetan Buddhism teaches that there are insights beyond shunyata—there is *prabhasvara* (luminosity) and *mahamudra* (the great symbol)—and the proper thing to do with any such experience is to explore it, then to let go and move on.[15] The responsibility of the teacher, then, is partly to give information, partly to help make sense of discoveries—which must be paid attention to, integrated—and partly to make sure you do not become complacent.

ENLIGHTENMENT involves a certain amount of cutting through attachments, a certain amount of unlearning of socially inculcated values and beliefs, and also a certain amount of what I can describe only as "regression"—getting down to levels of thought and feeling that are in some ways more primitive than ordinary consciousness.

This is another part of growth we all know about; in fact, it is one of the great recurrent themes of human experience, sounded again and again in legend, literature, scripture, psychology. Arthur Koestler has written of it as the key to creation and growth:

> . . . the perennial myth of the prophet's and hero's temporary isolation and retreat from human society, followed

by his triumphant return endowed with new powers. Buddha and Mohammed go out into the desert; Joseph is thrown into the well; Jesus is resurrected from the tomb. Jung's "death and rebirth" motif, Toynbee's "withdrawal and return" reflect the same archetypal motif . . . a principle of universal validity in the evolution of species, cultures, and individuals. . . .[16]

In describing this phenomenon, Koestler made use of the expression *"Reculer pour mieux sauter,"* "Step back to get ahead." It is the psychological concept of "regression in the service of the ego," and it is the rationale of the journey into infantile sexual fantasies that is undertaken in Freudian psychotherapy. It is also, of course, the basic principle underlying all the various schools of "dream analysis" that seek to recover, from our nightly journeys into the primitive psyche, something that can be integrated into our conscious understanding and help us to become more mature individuals.

This is an aspect of the enlightenment process that most people experience at some time or another. Somewhere along the way, usually just before a breakthrough is made, there is a regression into childhood memories or irresponsible behavior, perhaps a period of isolation (physical or emotional) from the rest of the world, or a phase of deep emotional depression, a withdrawal into what the Christian mystic St. John of the Cross called the "dark night of the soul." It takes many forms, and although such experiences are common, few of us have the wisdom or the good fortune to understand them as a part of growth, preludes to joy.

The Buddhist technology of growth includes many forms of regression, so many that some of its critics seem to think it is all retreat and no advance. Meditation, the most common feature of Buddhist practice, is in itself a retreat. It can be a brief respite for a few minutes in the day, or it can be a deliberate severing of connections with the world for several days, even, as in the case of some of the Tibetan practitioners, for several years. It can be a restful, nourishing withdrawal into passivity, or it can be a daring descent into the darkest depths of the psyche.

The elaborate visualization practices of the vajrayana are disciplined regression, in which the practitioner descends into the collective unconscious, contacts the archetypal images that most of us reveal to ourselves only in fairy tales and bad dreams and hallucinations, domesticates them, and makes them allies. These practices are among the most sophisticated forms of deep psychic self-exploration.

Still another kind of regression in the vajrayana tradition is the exploration of the preverbal strata of consciousness called *kun-ji*. This material is presented always with the assurance that you are not just being introduced to an interesting psychological concept but also being shown a way to descend into a mental space from which you will return with insight applicable to your everyday life.

Then there is the matter of experiencing the world without the ordinary (for most of us) sharp distinction between subject and object; this is repeatedly described in Buddhist writings as a desirable experience, if not the essence of enlightenment itself. But Western psychology tells us it is an infantile level of understanding; it is the psyche of the newborn baby who thinks the breast is a part of itself. Koestler describes the child's condition as "a liquid, fluid universe, traversed by psychological needs causing minor storms which come and go without leaving solid traces."[17]

Everything that we normally think of as growth is a matter of coming *out of* this universe, building a solid sense of what is "I" and what is "out there." When the individual fails to do this, he or she is fixed at some level of infantility, is certainly not a mature person and very likely not even regarded as a sane one. Yet this "liquid world," as Koestler calls it, continues to exist somewhere in the mature psyche; it can be dipped into again, and many people who do so report that the experience is not so much a descent into infan-

tile self-gratification as an *ascent* into a pure state of awareness, frequently described in religious terms. At a higher
level of maturity, something akin to the baby's universe is
discovered anew—and of course it had been there all the
time.

I HAVE BEEN SEARCHING for clues in the common
human experience that offer us some understanding of what
becoming enlightened is about, what we already *know* that
might be helpful in making Buddhism a little less inscrutable. We see that we do know a few things after all, as we
consider some of the experiences each of us has had at various stages of life.

We might also do well to consider what we know from
the history of *cultural* change, because when we look at how
societies evolve, we find something that resembles enlightenment; we see that they go through stages of redefining
some of their basic beliefs about the world. Nowadays this is
called "paradigm change," and we associate it with major
scientific theories that alter our view of reality. We usually
mark such changes with the names of people: Copernicus,
and the abandonment of the earth-centered universe; Dar-
win, and the view of an evolved (and evolving) human species; Freud, and the discovery (or rediscovery) of the
unconscious; Einstein, and the vision of a relativistic, non-
mechanistic cosmos in which matter is a form of energy. In
all such changes there are crises and breakthroughs. We
gain something, but we have to let go of something also; a
whole edifice of reality has to crumble every time we win a
wider understanding. We become wiser, but we also become more humble: Isn't there something like a loss of ego
in realizing that our little planet is not the center of the universe after all, that we are not set apart from the plant and
animal kingdoms, that many of our thoughts and actions are
shaped by unconscious mental processes, that the universe
is not simply a big piece of machinery operating according

to laws that we fully understand? We see those changes from this side, from our own time, and we know we have gained a wider horizon by letting some of those primitive beliefs slip away—but from the other side, it must have seemed impossible to exist without them.

Each time civilization passes through a major paradigm change, it has to let go of some old and rigidified concepts of humanity and the cosmos, concepts that do not seem to be concepts at all but simply the *truth*. Each time, there is powerful resistance to the change from those who find the new vision too frightening to contemplate; and each time, when the battle is more or less won, a certain smugness sets in: Now, at last, we've got it figured out. But it turns out that there is always another turn of the wheel, that today's wide new vista of the cosmos becomes tomorrow's set of barriers. And that is the image of *individual* human life that vajrayana Buddhism offers: an ever-widening circle of meaning, a qualitatively infinite cosmos. Enlightenment in the vajrayana is not a place; nor is it a single transcendent event in life. It is an ongoing process. There is no final nirvana.

All the therapies and spiritual trips that have been percolating through American society are parts of a paradigm shift, a still-incomplete effort to move beyond Darwinian and Freudian and behaviorist perspectives into a new and richer conceptualization of human life. There is no single central figure around whom this is organized, no Einstein of the mind. One voice we usually acknowledge is that of the late Abraham Maslow, an American writer well known to the Tibetans who have studied Western psychology. Maslow hoped to develop a psychology of health that would also provide the society with a meaningful ideal of personal development, something that people could understand and make part of their own lives.

Every age but ours has had its model, its ideal. All these have been given us by our culture; the saint, the hero, the gentleman, the knight, the mystic. About all we have left is the well-adjusted man without problems, a very pale and doubtful substitute. Perhaps we shall soon be able to use as our guide and model the fully growing and self-fulfilling human being, the one in whom all his potentialities are coming to full development, the one whose inner nature expresses itself fully freely, rather than being warped, suppressed, or denied.[18]

We mark the progression of Buddhism by its adoption of new guides and models. The hinayana had the *arhant*, a saintly but rather uptight paragon of Oriental virtue. The mahayana had the *bodhisattva*, a more human and accessible saint, whose greatest virtue was compassion. (Maslow noted that the healthy, self-actualized people he studied resembled the bodhisattva ideal—they had a natural, unfeigned concern for others, a felt sense of membership in the species.) The vajrayana retained the bodhisattva ideal as one rung on a ladder of development: ordinary people, bodhisattvas, yogis, siddhis, buddhas. This is an extraordinary vision of human possibilities that stretches Western beliefs to the breaking point—but note that for all its strangeness it remains a human system; it is not talking about God or gods but about human life, this life. It maintains that all people are potential buddhas and that all the possibilities of existence are present in ordinary consciousness. Even its deities are mind-beings, summoned up to serve as intermediaries between the individual consciousness and its environment. And its enlightenment is a learning process, different from other forms of adult education in that it requires periodic radical reformulation of all our ideas: letting go of old self-images, and forming new concepts of who and what we are. When a person does this, it is enlightenment; when a society does it, it is cultural transformation.

NONE OF THE IDEAS discussed here exactly explains enlightenment or proves that anybody ever experienced it; certainly there is no proof that further study or practice of Tibetan Buddhism will provide you with such an experience. I suggest only that the whole idea of Buddhism is not really so foreign to us as it may have appeared, that although we may not have such specifically Buddhist concepts as "nonself" and "impermanence" in our everyday language of life, there is much in our present knowledge—individual and collective—that tells us about such things.

And although I have been trying somewhat to "de-Orientalize" the idea of enlightenment, I have been working with ideas that are straight from the vajrayana tradition. Its clearest message is that enlightenment is not something to be apprehended from this or that tradition or teaching, although that may well help, but essentially something to be discovered in your own life. If it is alien to you, it is not enlightenment.

So although vajrayana Buddhism comes to us looking like a very exotic religion from a strange and distant land, it brings a message aimed directly at the innermost being of each of us.

It turns out that the real "diamond vehicle" is your own mind, rolling through time and reflecting all the brilliance of the universe. It may, it is true, be a bit mud-spattered with concepts of "self," rigid ideas, and hand-me-down beliefs, but nevertheless your mind—that one, the only one you know—is the inherently clear vehicle in which the truth is found. Whatever it is you are searching for—God, Buddha, yourself—is to be found there.

> So long as you do not recognize the Supreme One in
>   yourself,
> How should you gain this incomparable form?
> I have taught that when error ceases,
> You know yourself for what you are.
>
> He is at home, but she goes outside and looks.
> She sees her husband, but still asks the neighbors.
> Saraha says, O fool, know yourself.[19]

Appendix:
Kum-Nye Exercises

ALTHOUGH some of the kum-nye exercises are strenuous, they are basically for relaxation and relief of tension rather than for body-building. They may be done in conjunction with meditation (before or after a period of sitting meditation) or separately, as an aid to relaxation.

THE LION

Get down on "all fours"; in this case the "fours" are your knees and elbows. Try to keep your elbows together, and hold your hands in front of you. Make both hands into fists, and hold them together in front of you, touching but not interlaced. Raise your feet off the floor, point the toes, look up so that the neck is stretched. Your upper back is rounded; stomach muscles are pulled in. To make the exercise more strenuous, move your elbows farther forward. For beginners, a couple of minutes is fine; later you may be able to hold the position for a longer time.

ENERGIZER

Bend forward, touch your hands to the floor, and exhale. (The knees should not be locked, and can be allowed to bend slightly.) Inhale as you come back up. Do this exercise rapidly, keeping your movements coordinated with the breath. This is a good warmup for the "hah" exercises.

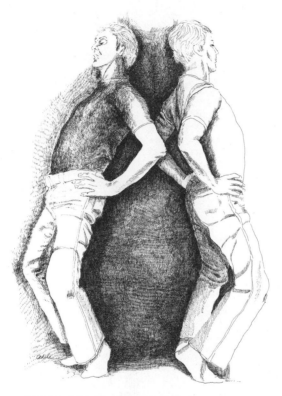

DIAMOND POSTURE (*vajrasana*)

This is one of the most powerful of the kum-nye exercises, and an effective way to release emotional tension. Stand with hands on hips, feet pointed outward, and raise up onto the toes, keeping the heels close together. Extend the pelvis forward. Breathe deeply and slowly, and hold the posture for at least five minutes.

MOVING MEDITATION

Begin by bringing the hands together over the center of the chest, fingers interlaced. Keeping the fingers interlaced, stretch upward, palms up, inhaling deeply. Release the fingers and exhale slowly and gently as the hands come downward. Bring the hands back to the chest center and begin again. Continue the meditation for at least five minutes, eyes closed, moving the arms in time with the breath.

FRONT "HAH"

Sit in a comfortable cross-legged position and extend the arms out to the sides and fold the hands as follows: First tuck the thumb in against the palm, and fold the ring finger across it, then the middle finger, then the index finger, and finally the little finger. Bring the fists together at the center of the chest, holding the fists tightly and pressing them against the chest. Inhale deeply and hold your breath. Then, in a single vigorous motion, fling the arms straight out to the sides and give a "hah" shout. Fold the hands into fists again, and repeat two more times. Rest the hands on the lap for a minute, breathing easily, then begin again. Do the exercise a total of 9 times, in sets of 3. This exercise is meant to be done in the afternoon or late in the day.

BALANCE

Balance (the "middle way") is one of the major themes of Buddhism, and this simple exercise becomes surprisingly meaningful if you use it as a meditation on balance—that is,

if you think about balance and what it means to your own life while you are doing it. Stand with the hands on the hips and raise one leg, with the knee bent and toes pointed upward. Hold for a few minutes, then repeat with the other leg. Then you can move into variations and improvisations on the basic exercise. Try extending the hands out to the sides and moving the arms horizontally, front to back; then try moving the arms up and down and stretching the torso from side to side as you stand on one foot. Finally, experiment with moving the free leg to the side or backward, as in the second drawing.

ARM ROTATIONS

Sit in a comfortable cross-legged position. With each hand, grasp the pectoral muscle between the thumb and index finger. Rotate the arms, swinging the elbows up, back, down, and forward. Repeat several times, and then reverse the rotation.

PUNCH AND JUMP

(*opposite*)

Stand, with your feet at about shoulder width. Your weight should be equally distributed. With a quick jump, step forward with the left foot and backward with the right. At the same time, straighten your right arm, fist clenched, in front of you, and draw back the left arm so the left fist is at about waist level. With another jump, reverse the position: right foot forward, left foot back, right arm back, left arm forward. Repeat this 15 or 20 times, and turn about 45 degrees with each jump, eventually completing a full circle.

SWIM

Sit in a comfortable cross-legged position and stretch one arm forward, turning the upper body at the same time and stretching the other arm backward. Then turn the upper body and do the same motion to the other side. Repeat several times, in a long, slow motion, with full stretches.

SIDE STRETCH

With a wide stance, hands on hips, step far forward with one foot, keeping the back leg straight. Bend to one side and then the other, far enough to get a good stretch each way. Reverse the stance, and repeat.

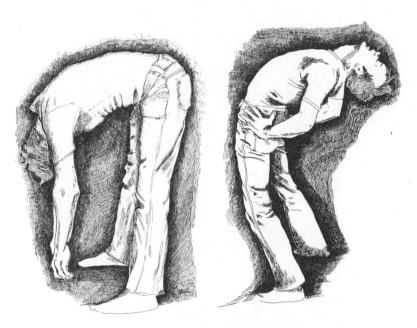

HANG AND BACK BEND

Stand, with the feet at shoulder width, and bend forward so that the arms and head hang down. Allow your body to relax into the position; breathe deeply, letting the arms and head swing gently with the body's motion. Hold for a few minutes and then bend backward, putting your hands against the buttocks or small of the back for support. Bend the knees slightly and drop the head back. Gently move the upper body, letting yourself bend farther backward. Bend forward again and continue until you have done the full sequence at least 3 times. Then stand with your eyes closed and breathe easily.

FULL BODY STRETCH

Step well forward, keeping the back leg straight and lifting the heel of the forward foot. Clasp your hands at the back of the neck. Look upward, letting the elbows fall back so that you feel the stretch in the muscles of the shoulders and chest. Go as far into the stretch as you can, then do the same thing with the foot positions reversed. Afterward, bend forward and let the head and arms hang downward as in the hang and back bend.

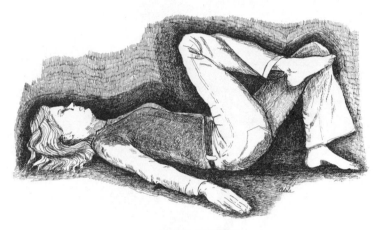

LEG LIFTS

Lie on the floor, on a mat or soft carpet. Hands are out to the sides of the body, palms down, relaxed. Knees are raised, and soles of both feet flat on the floor. Just lie in this position for a while, letting the breath become regular, slow, and deep. Then, as you begin an exhalation, slowly raise the right foot off the floor. Raise the heel first, so that the toes are the last part of the foot touching the floor. Continue raising the leg as you exhale, until the knee is close to your chest. Then, as you inhale, return the right foot to the floor—touching the floor first with the toes, then lowering the heel. As you begin another exhalation, slowly raise the left leg. Repeat the entire cycle several times, allowing the breath and the motion to become slow and smooth.

SIDE "HAH"

In a seated position, move the hands toward one side, turning the body slightly, and then quickly extend both hands toward the side in a pushing motion, giving a shout of "hah" with the push. With a gentle inhalation, bring the hands to the other side and do the same thing. Do this 3 times to each side. This is a good exercise for releasing feelings of anger or frustration, and some people find they can get into it better by thinking about a specific person or situation that causes the feelings. Try thinking about pushing something away, making space for yourself to relax. The push and shout can be made very intense if that feels right for you.

STANDING MEDITATION

Stand comfortably and stretch the arms above the head, as if you were holding a large ball in your hands and trying to get it as high as possible. As you reach upward, imagine your entire body expanding, becoming lighter, as if you were being pulled upward by your hands. Hold the position for a few minutes with the stretch extended as far as possible, then slowly bring the hands together over the center of the chest and stand with your eyes closed.

Glossary

ANATMAN—no soul; nonself.

ARHANT—a saint who has triumphed over desire through virtue and willpower.

ASURAS—demigods of the wheel of life.

BARDOS—planes or states of existence after death.

CETANA—volition.

CHAKRA—a center in the body; the locus of certain properties.

DHARMAS—the basic elements of mental process; *dharma* is also a general term for the totality of Buddhist teachings.

DUKKA—unsatisfactoriness; the first noble truth.

HINAYANA—the "lesser vehicle"; early schools of Buddhism.

JNANA—mature wisdom; knowledge by experience.

KARMA—action and its consequences; cause and effect.

KARUNA—compassion.

KUM NYE—a system of relaxation exercise.

KUN-JI—the ground-state below thoughts.

LUNG-GOM—trance walk.

MAHAYANA—the "greater vehicle"; later form of Buddhism.

MANAS—thought; the sixth sense; the subjective operation of processing sense data.

MANASKARA—attention; application.

MANDALA—an arrangement of symbols, used as a visual meditation device.

MANTRA—a phrase or sound used in meditation.

MARGA—path; the fourth noble truth.

MUDRA—a physical posture or gesture, especially of the hands.

NIRODHA—extinction; the third noble truth.

NIRVANA—enlightenment.

PRAJNA—discriminating wisdom; ability to achieve a clear and precise awareness of any situation.

PRETAS—hungry ghosts of the wheel of life.

SAMADHI—concentration; meditation.

SAMANVAYA—the act of reconciling contrary beliefs.

SAMJNA—activity of classifying and defining.

SAMSARA—going around in circles; the suffering consciousness; the cycle of death and rebirth.

SAMUDAYA—cause or origin; the second noble truth.

SANGHA—the community or order of Buddhists.

SANG-YAS—Tibetan term for a *buddha.*

SARVATRANGA—"going everywhere"; omnipresent mental events.

SHIN JONG—a state of "higher alertness" or "natural awareness."

SHUNYATA—emptiness; "no-thing-ness."

SIDDHIS—powers.

SKANDHA—one of the five aggregates or categories of dharmas; basic constituents of the personality, usually identified as feelings, perceptions, impulses, consciousness, form.

SPARSA—rapport; contact.

SURAS—gods of the wheel of life.

SUTRAS—the teachings of Lord Gautama.

TANTRA—a text; a spiritual tradition which stresses the interconnectedness of all things, and which in some places involves secret teachings and the use of mantras, mandalas, and mudras.

TUMO—mystic heat.

VAJRAYANA—the "diamond vehicle"; Buddhism based on the Tantric tradition.

VEDANA—feeling-tone.

Notes

Preface

1. Herbert Fingarette, "The Ego and Mystic Selflessness," in *Identity and Anxiety*, ed. Maurice Stein, Arthur J. Vidich, and David Manning White (Glencoe, Ill.: The Free Press, 1960), pp. 552–581.
2. L. A. Waddell, *The Buddhism of Tibet, or Lamaism* (Cambridge: W. Heffer and Sons, 1971), pp. xv, 145.

1. East Is East, and West Is West

1. Theodore Roszak, *The Making of a Counter-Culture* (New York: Doubleday, 1969).
2. See Bernard Gunther, *Sensory Awakening: Below Your Mind* (New York: Macmillan, 1968).
3. One well-done example of this kind of scholarship is Stephan Beyer's *The Cult of Tara: Magic and Ritualism in Tibet* (Berkeley: University of California Press, 1973).
4. Lawrence Kohlberg, "Stages and Sequence: The Cognitive-

Developmental Approach to Socialization," in *Handbook of Socialization Theory and Research,* ed. David A. Godlin (Chicago: Rand, McNally, 1960), p. 347.

5. Abraham Maslow, *Toward a Psychology of Being* (New York: Van Nostrand, 1962). This concept is also taken up in Charles Hampden-Turner, *Radical Man* (New York: Doubleday, 1971).
6. Lewis Mumford, *The Myth of the Machine,* vol. 1, *Technics and Human Development* (New York: Harcourt, Brace & World, 1967), pp. 7–9.

2. Buddhist Basics

1. Niccolò Machiavelli, *The Discourses* (New York: Modern Library, 1940), p. 208.
2. From the Kalama Sutra, in *Buddhism,* Alexandra David-Neel (London: John Lane the Bodley Head, 1939; and New York: St. Martin's Press, 1939), p. 123.
3. From the Potthapada Sutra, in *The Wisdom of Buddhism,* ed. Christmas Humphries (London: Rider, 1961), pp. 53–54.
4. Arnold Beisser, "The Paradoxical Theory of Change," in *Gestalt Therapy Now,* ed. Joen Fagan and Irma Lee Shepherd (New York: Harper & Row, 1970), p. 77. (Italics in original.)
5. Lama Mi-pham, *Calm and Clear,* tr. Herbert V. Guenther (Berkeley: Dharma Publishing, 1973), pp. 43, 49.
6. Walpola Rahula, *What the Buddha Taught* (Bedford, England: Gordon Fraser, 1959), p. 66.
7. David-Neel, *Buddhism,* pp. 130–131.
8. Erich Fromm, D. T. Suzuki, and Richard De Martino, *Zen Buddhism and Psychoanalysis* (New York: Harper & Row, 1970), p. 99.
9. Nolan Jacobson, *Buddhism: The Religion of Analysis* (London: George Allen & Unwin, 1966), pp. 133–134.
10. Some of these ideas are discussed by Alexandra David-Neel in *The Secret Oral Teachings* (San Francisco: City Lights, 1967), a book the late Alan Watts, no admirer of the standard idea of reincarnation, used to call the "I-told-you-so book."
11. Herbert V. Guenther, *Treasures on the Tibetan Middle Way* (Berkeley: Shambhala, 1973), p. 45.
12. Anonymous, quoted in Agehananda Bharati, *The Tantric Tradition* (Garden City, N.Y.: Anchor, 1970), p. 19. (Italics in source.)

3. *Your Mind: Now You See It, Now You Don't*

1. Ye-shes rgyal-mtshan, *The Necklace of Clear Understanding*, tr. H. V. Guenther and Leslie Kawamura and published under the title *Mind in Buddhist Psychology* (Berkeley: Dharma Publishing, 1975), p. 20.
2. C. G. Jung, *Psychological Types*, tr. H. G. Baynes, revised by R. F. C. Hull (Princeton, N.J.: Princeton University Press, 1971), p. 434. (Italics in source.)
3. Ye-shes rgyal-mtshan, p. 25.
4. From the Prajna-paramita-hridaya Sutra, in *The Wisdom of Buddhism*, ed. Christmas Humphries (London: Rider, 1961), p. 114.

4. *Vajrayana: The Diamond Vehicle*

1. Quoted in Edward Conze, *Buddhism: Its Essence and Development*, tr. C. R. Lanman, 1901 (New York: Harper & Bros., 1951). Translation revised by author.
2. *Cittavisuddhiprakarana*, vols. 37, 38, in *Buddhist Texts Through the Ages*, ed. Edward Conze, tr. David Snellgrove (New York: Harper & Row, 1964), p. 221.
3. Quoted in Bharati, p. 20. See also Helmuth von Glasnapp, *Buddhism: A Non-Theistic Religion*, tr. Irmgard Schlogel (New York: Braziller, 1966).
4. S. B. Dasgupta, *An Introduction to Tantric Buddhism* (Berkeley: Shambala, 1974), p. 3.
5. Longchenpa, *Kindly Bent to Ease Us*, tr. Herbert V. Guenther (Berkeley: Dharma Press, 1975), part I: "Mind," p. 100.
6. "Our Mind . . . is no peacefully self-contained unity. It is rather to be compared with a modern State in which a mob, eager for enjoyment and destruction, has to be held down forcibly by a prudent superior class." Sigmund Freud, "My Contact with Josef Popper-Lynkeus," 1932, in Philip Rieff (ed.), *Character and Culture*, tr. James Strachey (New York: Crowell-Collier, 1963), p. 303.
7. The English terms vary. These are the ones used by John Blofeld in *The Tantric Mysticism of Tibet* (New York: E. P. Dutton, 1970), pp. 80–83.
8. See Stephan Beyer, *The Cult of Tara: Magic and Ritualism in*

Tibet (Berkeley: University of California Press, 1973).

9. Lama Anagarika Govinda, *Foundations of Tibetan Mysticism* (New York: Samuel Weiser, 1973).

10. Blofeld, pp. 118–119.

11. One of the best pieces on this subject is Nathan Katz's "Anima and mKa'-'gro-ma: A Critical Comparative Study of Jung and Tibetan Buddhism," *The Tibet Journal*, vol. II, no. 3, Autumn 1977, pp. 13–43.

12. C. G. Jung, *Two Essays in Analytic Psychology* (Princeton: Princeton University Press, 1972), p. 201.

13. Beyer, pp. 83–84.

14. C. G. Jung, "Psychological Commentary," in *The Tibetan Book of the Dead*, ed. W. Y. Evans-Wentz, tr. R. F. C. Hull (New York: Oxford University Press, 1957), p. xxxviii.

5. The Body on the Spiritual Path: Relaxation, Health, and Healing

1. M. Friedman and R. H. Rosenman, *Type A Behavior and Your Heart* (New York: Knopf, 1974). Quoted in Kenneth Pelletier, *Mind as Healer, Mind as Slayer* (New York: Delta, 1977), p. 126.

2. Pelletier, Ch. 6. Findings specifically related to transcendental meditation are summarized in Harold H. Bloomfield, Michael Peter Cain, and Dennis T. Jaffe, *TM: Discovering Inner Energy and Overcoming Stress* (New York: Delacorte, 1975).

3. Yesehe Dhonden and Gyatsho Tshering, "What Is Tibetan Medicine?" in *An Introduction to Tibetan Medicine*, ed. Dawa Norbu (New Delhi: *Tibetan Review*, 1976), p. 7.

4. Pelletier, pp. 110–111.

5. Jampal Kunzang Rechung, Rinpoche, *Tibetan Medicine* (Berkeley: University of California Press, 1973), p. 58.

6. Dhonden and Tshering, p. 7.

7. Theodore Burang, "Tibetan Medicine on Cancer," in *An Introduction to Tibetan Medicine*, ed. Dawa Norbu (New Delhi: *Tibetan Review*, 1976), p. 60.

6. The Expanding Universe and the Expanding Mind

1. A. J. Singh, "Interview with the Dalai Lama," *Tibet Journal*, vol. II, no. 3, Autumn 1977, pp. 8–12.

220   *Notes*

2. Alan Watts, *Psychotherapy East and West* (New York: Pantheon, 1961).
3. Watts; see especially p. ix.
4. Fritjof Capra, *The Tao of Physics* (New York: Bantam, 1977), pp. 3–4.
5. From Isaac Newton, *Opticks,* quoted in *The Science of Matter,* ed. M. P. Crossland (Harmondsworth, England: Penguin, 1971), p. 76.
6. A. N. Whitehead, *Science and the Modern World* (New York: Macmillan, 1926), p. 84.
7. Thomas Kuhn, *The Structure of Scientific Revolutions* (Chicago: Chicago University Press, 1970).
8. Einstein's theory was not a direct consequence of the Michelson-Morley experiments, as it is sometimes said to have been. Although the experiments did provide some support for Einstein, his theory came from his own speculative thinking. See Michael Polanyi, *Personal Knowledge* (Chicago: University of Chicago Press, 1962), pp. 9–12.
9. Capra, p. 50.
10. T. and D. McKenna, *The Invisible Landscape* (New York: Seabury Press, 1975), pp. 32–33.
11. E. P. Tryon, "Is the Universe a Vacuum Fluctuation?" *Nature,* December 1973, pp. 396–397.
12. David Bohm, *Causality and Chance in Modern Physics* (London: Routledge & Kegan Paul, 1957), p. 153.
13. Werner Heisenberg, *Physics and Philosophy* (New York: Harper & Row, 1962), p. 81.
14. From the Surangama Sutra, in *A Buddhist Bible,* ed. Dwight Goddard, tr. Bhikshu Wai-tao and Dwight Goddard (New York: E. P. Dutton, 1938), p. 243.
15. Quoted in *The Wisdom of Buddhism,* ed. Christmas Humphries (London: Rider, 1961), p. 218.
16. Quoted in Kennard Lipman, "The Meaning of 'World' in Tibetan Buddhist Philosophy," unpublished Master of Arts dissertation, University of Saskatchewan, 1976.
17. Lipman.
18. See, for example, Gampopa, *Jewel Ornament of Liberation,* tr. Herbert V. Guenther (Berkeley: Shambhala, 1971), pp. 212–226.

19. Herbert V. Guenther and Chögyam Trungpa, *The Dawn of Tantra* (Berkeley: Shambhala, 1975), p. 34.

20. Guenther and Trungpa, p. 35.

21. Lipman.

22. Guenther and Trungpa, p. 82.

23. Karl Pribram, "Toward a Holonomic Theory of Perception," *Gestalttheorie in der modernen Psychologie* (1975), p. 184.

24. "Theoretical Physics Must Deal with Thought—Bohm," *Brain/Mind Bulletin*, September 19, 1977, p. 2.

7. Dream Analysis, Tibetan Style

1. Gen. 41:16.

2. Sigmund Freud, *The Interpretation of Dreams*, in *The Basic Writings of Sigmund Freud*, tr. A. A. Brill (New York: Modern Library, 1938), p. 184.

3. Freud, p. 223.

4. C. G. Jung, *Memories, Dreams, Reflections*, tr. Richard and Clara Winston (New York: Vintage, 1962), p. 161.

5. Jung, *Memories, Dreams, Reflections*, p. 138.

6. C. G. Jung, *Collected Works, Vol. 10: Civilization in Transition* (Princeton: Princeton University Press, 1967), p. 847.

7. Frederick S. Perls, "Dream Seminars," in Fagan and Shepherd, pp. 213–214.

8. *Chuang Tzu, Book II*, quoted in Stanley Krippner and William Hughes, "Dreams and Human Potential," *Journal of Humanistic Psychology*, vol. X, no. 1, Spring 1970, p. 1.

9. René Descartes, "Meditation 1," in *The Philosophical World of Descartes*, tr. Elizabeth Haldane and G. R. T. Ross (Cambridge: Cambridge University Press, 1911), p. 146.

10. Descartes, p. 145.

11. In Charles E. M. Dunlop (ed.), *Philosophical Essays on Dreaming* (Ithaca, N.Y.: Cornell University Press), pp. 103–126.

12. Charles H. Tart, "The 'High' Dream: A New State of Consciousness," in *Altered States of Consciousness* (New York: Wiley, 1969), p. 170.

13. Garma Chang, *Teachings of Tibetan Yoga* (Secaucus, New Jersey: Citadel Press, 1977), p. 92. The material on dream yoga in this chapter of Chang's book is translated from writings by Lama

Drashi Nanjah Namjhal, based on the teachings of Naropa, the eleventh-century Indian teacher who is associated with the Kagyu school of Tibetan Buddhism.

14. Tart, p. 174.
15. Krippner and Hughes, p. 15.
16. Chang, p. 90.
17. Longchenpa, *Kindly Bent to Ease Us*, part 3: "Wonderment," tr. Herbert V. Guenther (Berkeley: Dharma Press, 1976), p. 44.
18. Tarthang Tulku, *Crystal Mirror*, vol. IV (Berkeley: Dharma Publishing, 1975), p. 181.

8. Rumors from the East

1. Pantanjali, *How to Know God: The Yoga Aphorisms of Patanjali*, tr. Swami Prabhavananda and Christopher Isherwood (New York: Mentor, 1969), p. 126.
2. Alexandra David-Neel, *Magic and Mystery in Tibet* (New York: Penguin, 1971), pp. 202–203.
3. Lama Govinda, *The Way of the White Clouds* (Berkeley: Shambhala, 1970), pp. 77–78.
4. David-Neel, p. 227. The word *respa* is the title of the tumo adepts; it refers to the light cotton robe worn by them in all weather.
5. Milarepa, quoted in David-Neel, p. 224.
6. Some of the books that discuss the tumo practice are Garma Chang's *Teachings of a Tibetan Yoga*, David-Neel's *Magic and Mystery in Tibet*, Govinda's *Foundations of Tibetan Mysticism*, and Guenther's *The Life and Teachings of Naropa*.
7. Elmer Green, "Biofeedback Training and Yoga," a paper presented at the Association for Humanistic Psychology conference on psychic healing, San Francisco, May 1972.
8. Mike Spino, *Beyond Jogging* (Millbrae, Calif.: Celestial Arts, 1976).
9. George B. Leonard, *The Ultimate Athlete* (New York: Viking, 1975).
10. W. Y. Evans-Wentz, *The Tibetan Book of the Dead*, tr. Lama Dawa-Samdup (New York: Oxford University Press, 1977).
11. Evans-Wentz, p. 96.
12. Evans-Wentz, p. 98.
13. Evans-Wentz, pp. 121–122.

14. Evans-Wentz, p. 179.
15. Evans-Wentz, p. xxxvii. (The third edition of *The Tibetan Book of the Dead* cited here contains the commentaries by Jung and Lama Govinda.)
16. Evans-Wentz, pp. lix–lxi.
17. Evans-Wentz, p. liii.
18. Timothy Leary, Ralph Metzner, and Richard Alpert, *The Psychedelic Experience* (New Hyde Park, N.Y.: University Books, 1964), p. 22.
19. Leary, Metzner, and Alpert, p. 31.
20. Raymond Moody, *Life After Life* (New York: Bantam, 1976), pp. 21–22.

9. More Tibetan Psychology:
The Wheel of Life, the Higher Alertness, and the Ground of Being

1. Herbert V. Guenther, *The Tantric View of Life* (Boulder, Colorado: Shambhala, 1976), p. 38.
2. Longchenpa, *Kindly Bent to Ease Us*, part III: "Wonderment," *op. cit.*, p. 106.
3. Longchenpa, part I, p. 113.
4. Tarthang Tulku, *Crystal Mirror*, vol. IV, p. 166.
5. Tarthang Tulku, "The Pursuit of Awareness," *Gesar*, Spring 1975, p. 4. (Published by Dharma Publishing, Berkeley, California.)
6. Gay Luce, "Western Psychology Meets Tibetan Buddhism," in *Reflections of Mind*, ed. Tarthang Tulku (Berkeley, California: Dharma Publishing, 1975), p. 36.

10. Enlightenment: Learning and Unlearning

1. Herbert V. Guenther, *Jewel Ornament of Liberation*, p. 207.
2. See Chögyam Trungpa's comments on this in Trungpa and Guenther, *The Dawn of Tantra*, p. 82.
3. Cor. 13:11.
4. Herbert Fingarette, in *Identity and Anxiety*, p. 553.
5. Fingarette, p. 554.
6. Fingarette, p. 555.

7. "Saraha's Treasury of Songs," in *Buddhist Texts Through the Ages*, p. 234.
8. Guenther, *Jewel Ornament of Liberation*, p. 222.
9. Fingarette, p. 569.
10. Nolan P. Jacobson, *Buddhism: The Religion of Analysis*, p. 84.
11. Jacobson, p. 101.
12. Shuuryu Suzuki, quoted in Arthur Deikman, *Personal Freedom* (New York: Viking, 1976), p. 31.
13. Guenther, p. 241.
14. Guenther, p. 212.
15. Guenther and Trungpa, *The Dawn of Tantra*, p. 35.
16. Arthur Koestler, *The Act of Creation* (New York: Macmillan, 1964), p. 466.
17. Arthur Koestler, "The Three Domains of Creativity," in *Challenges of Humanistic Psychology*, ed. F. T. Bugenthal (New York: McGraw-Hill, 1967), p. 35.
18. Maslow, p. 4.
19. In Edward Conze (ed.), *Buddhist Texts Through the Ages*, p. 232.

Index